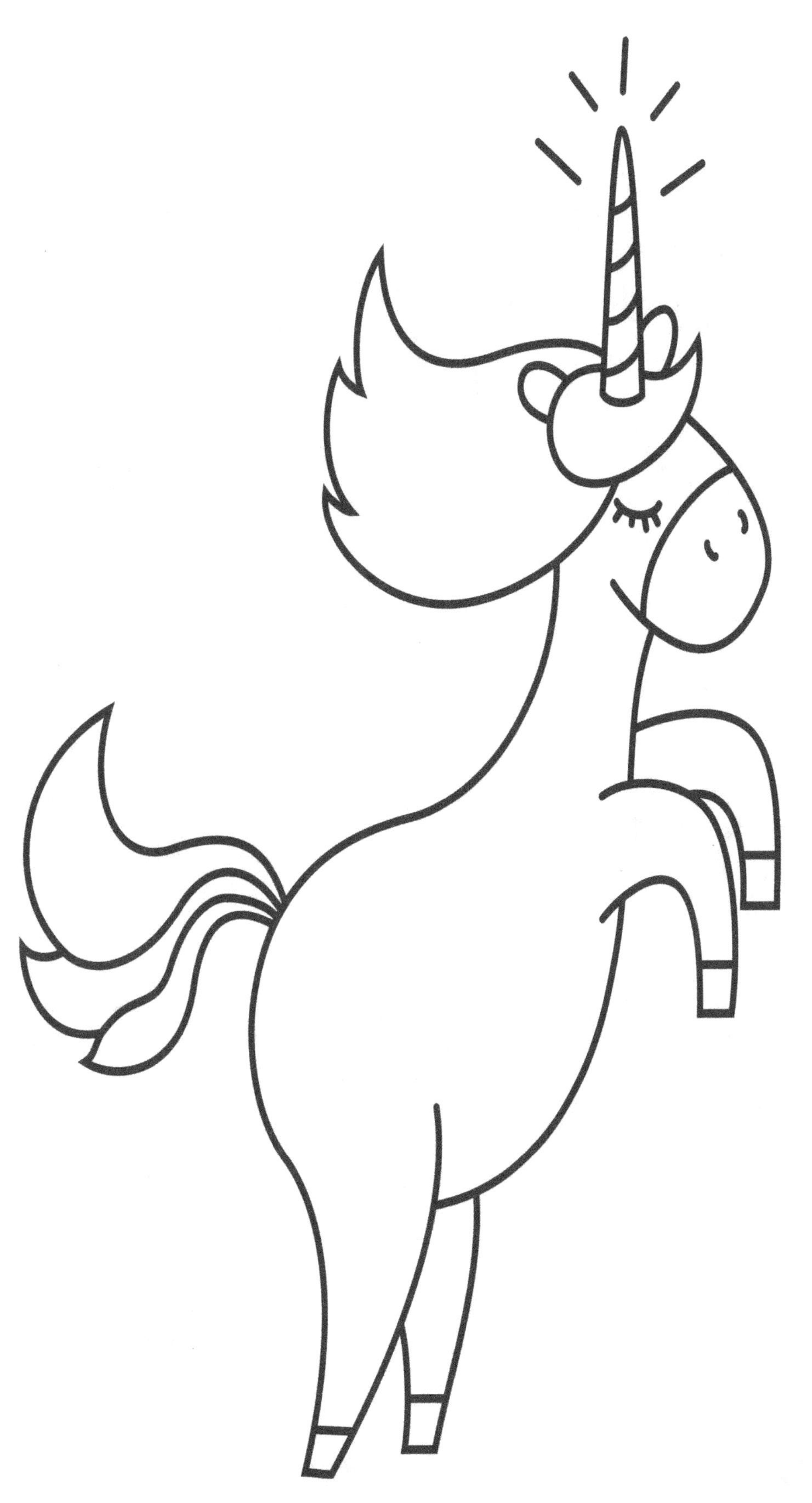

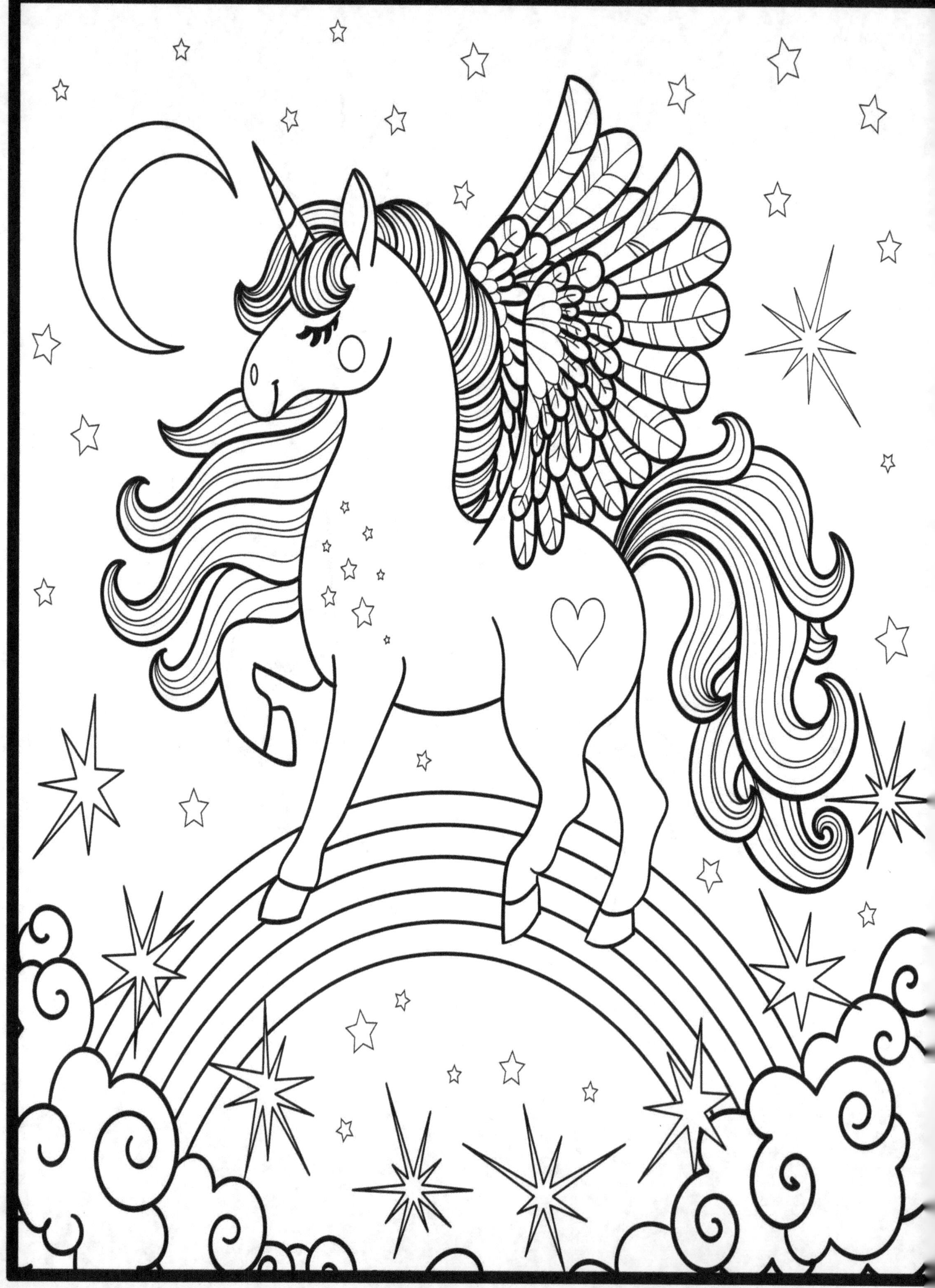

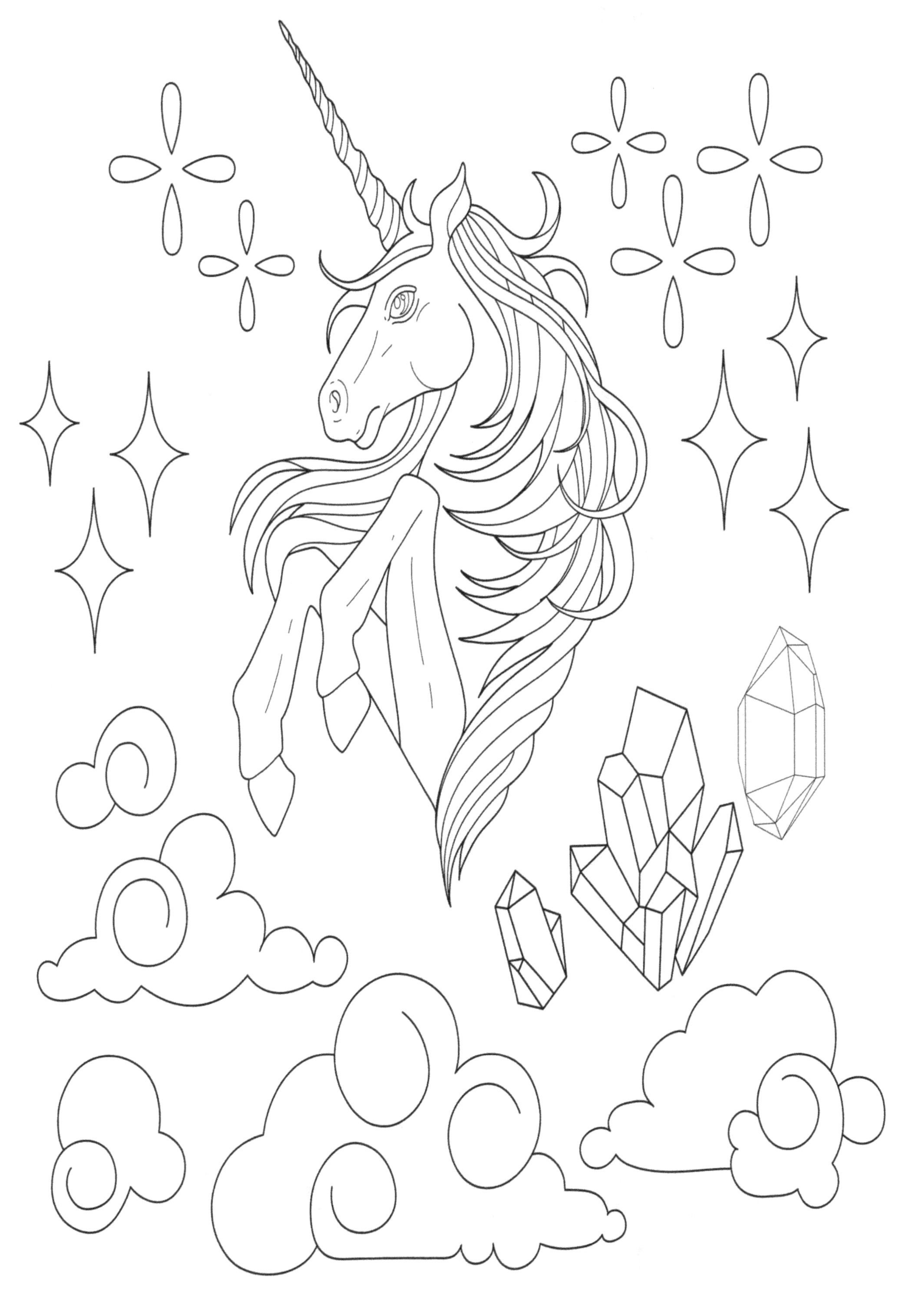

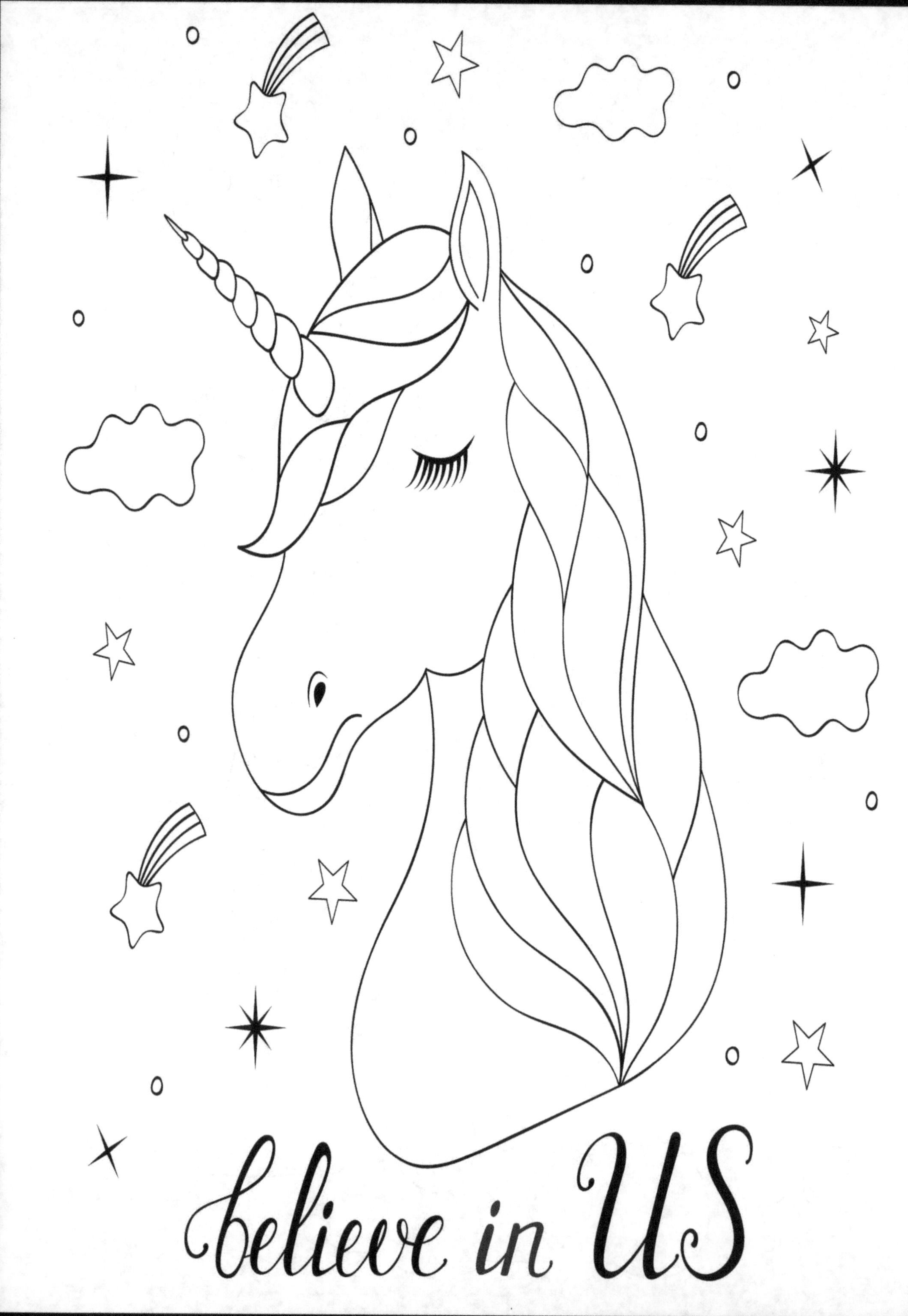
believe in US

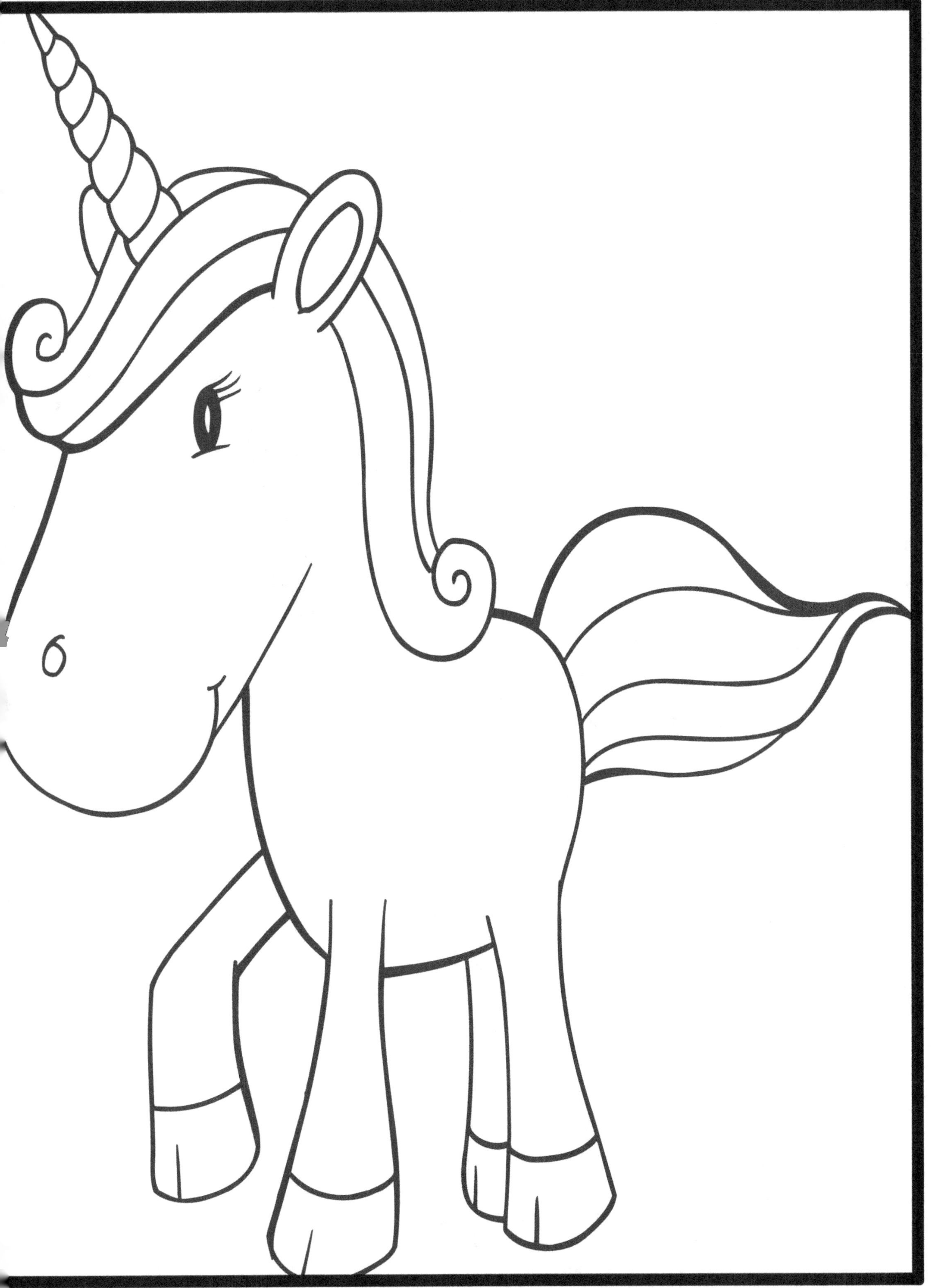

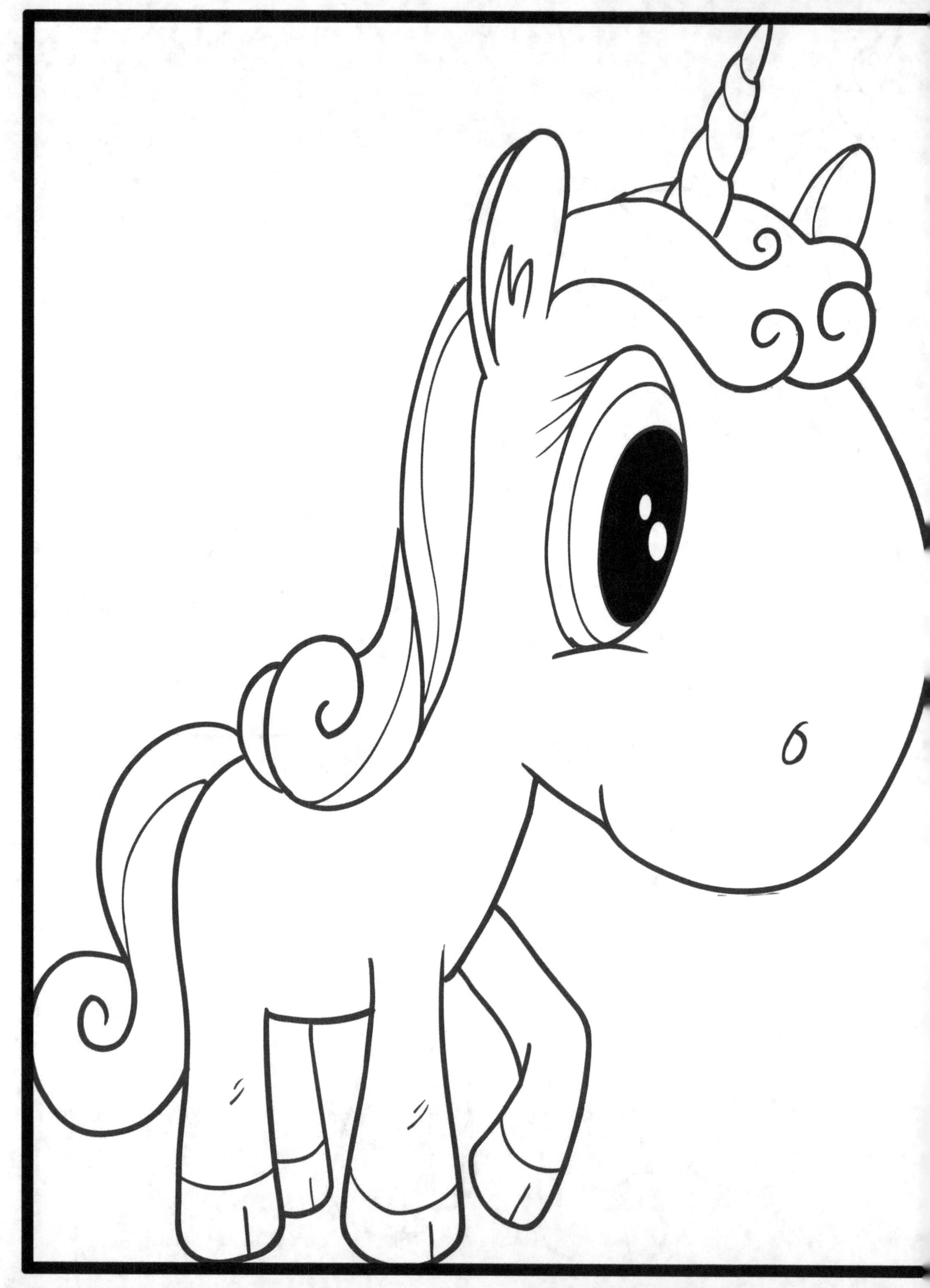

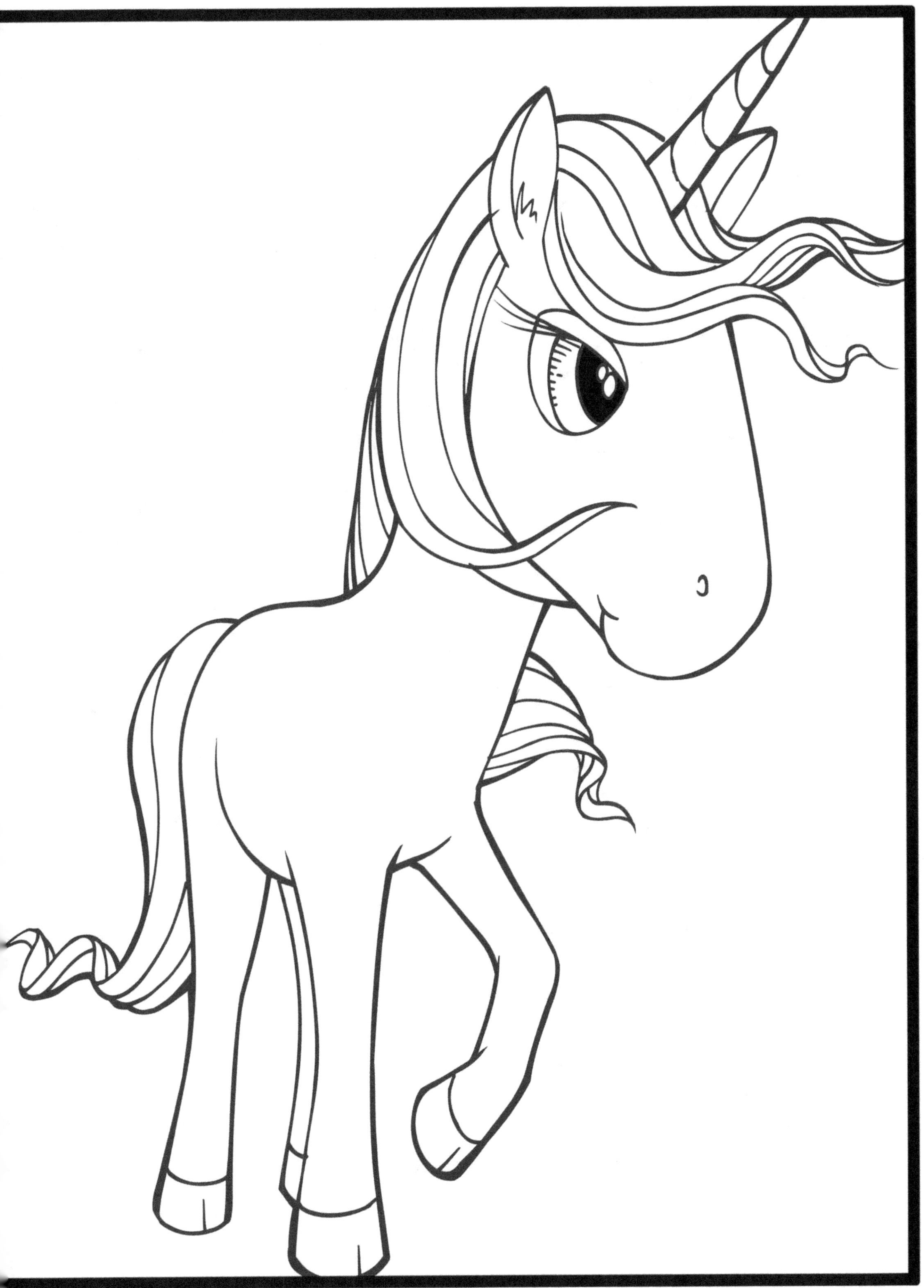

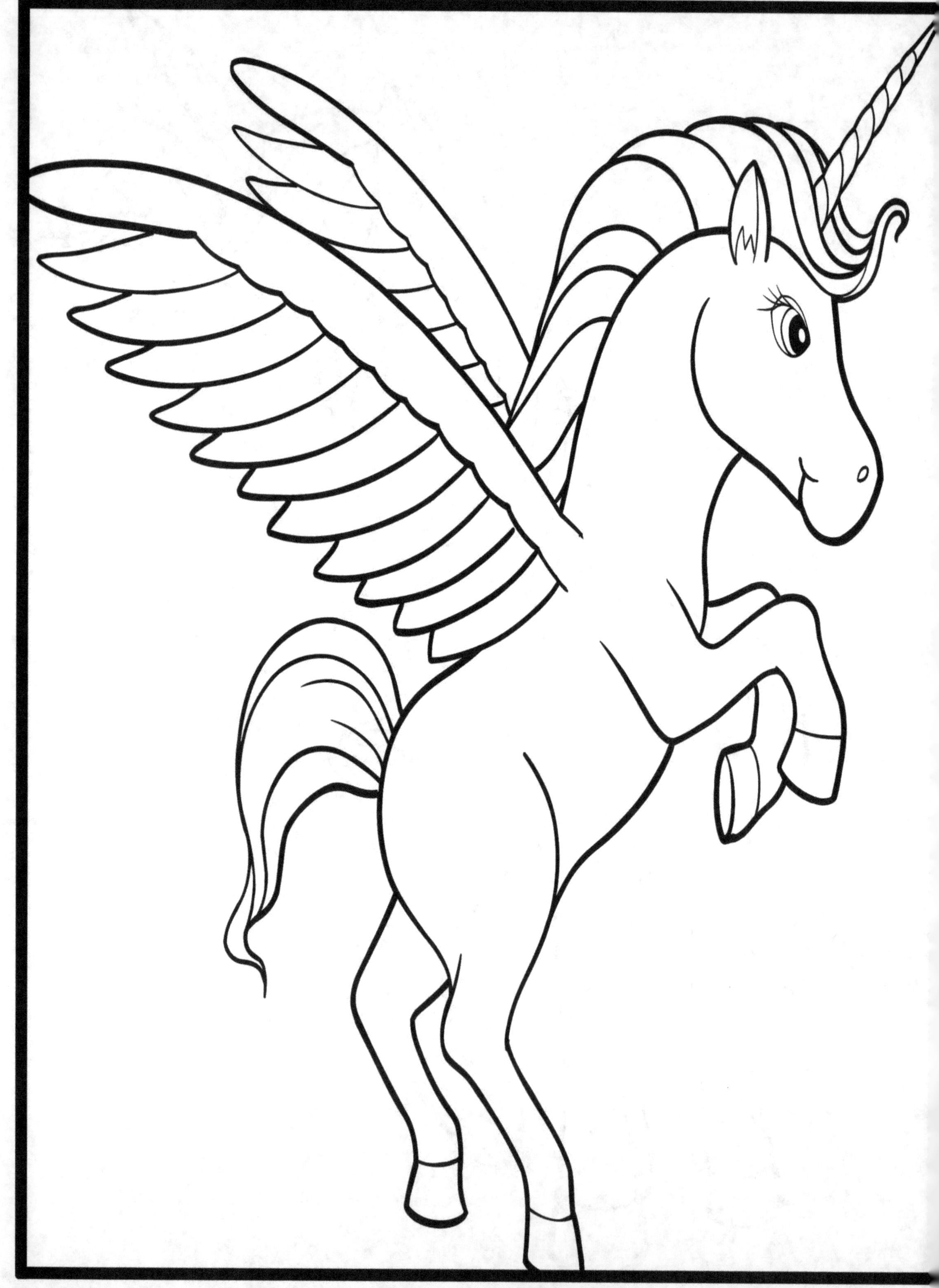

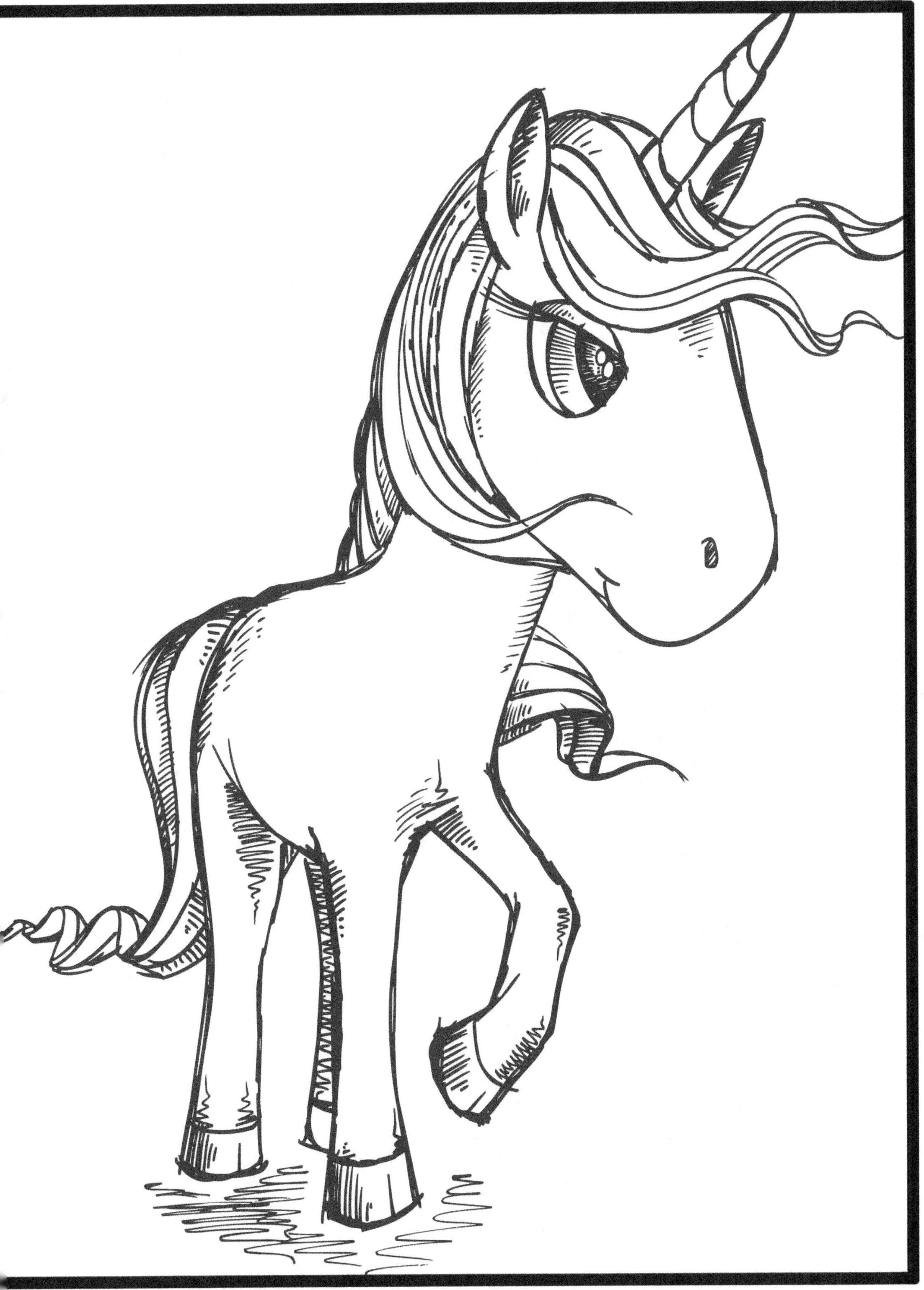

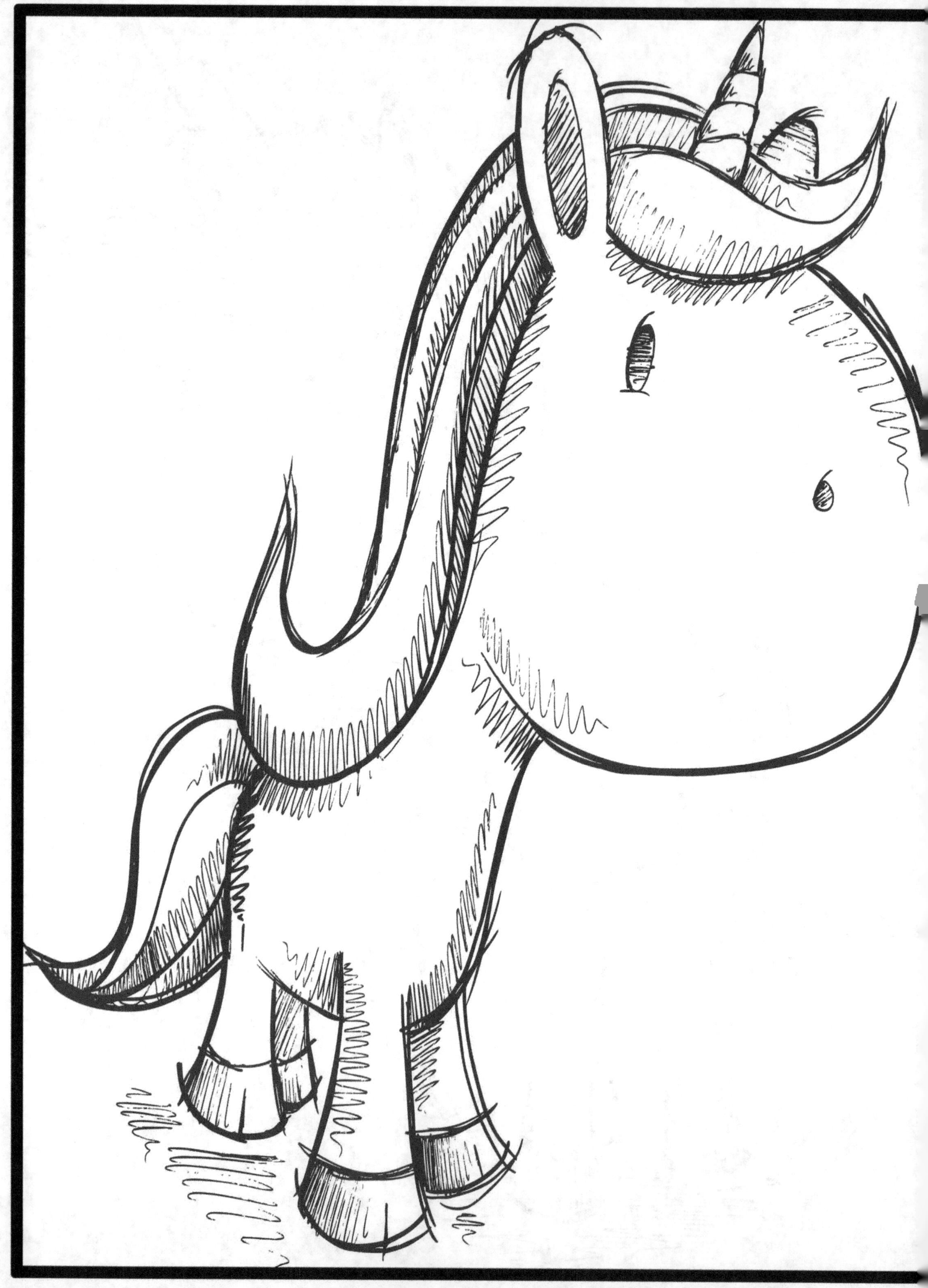

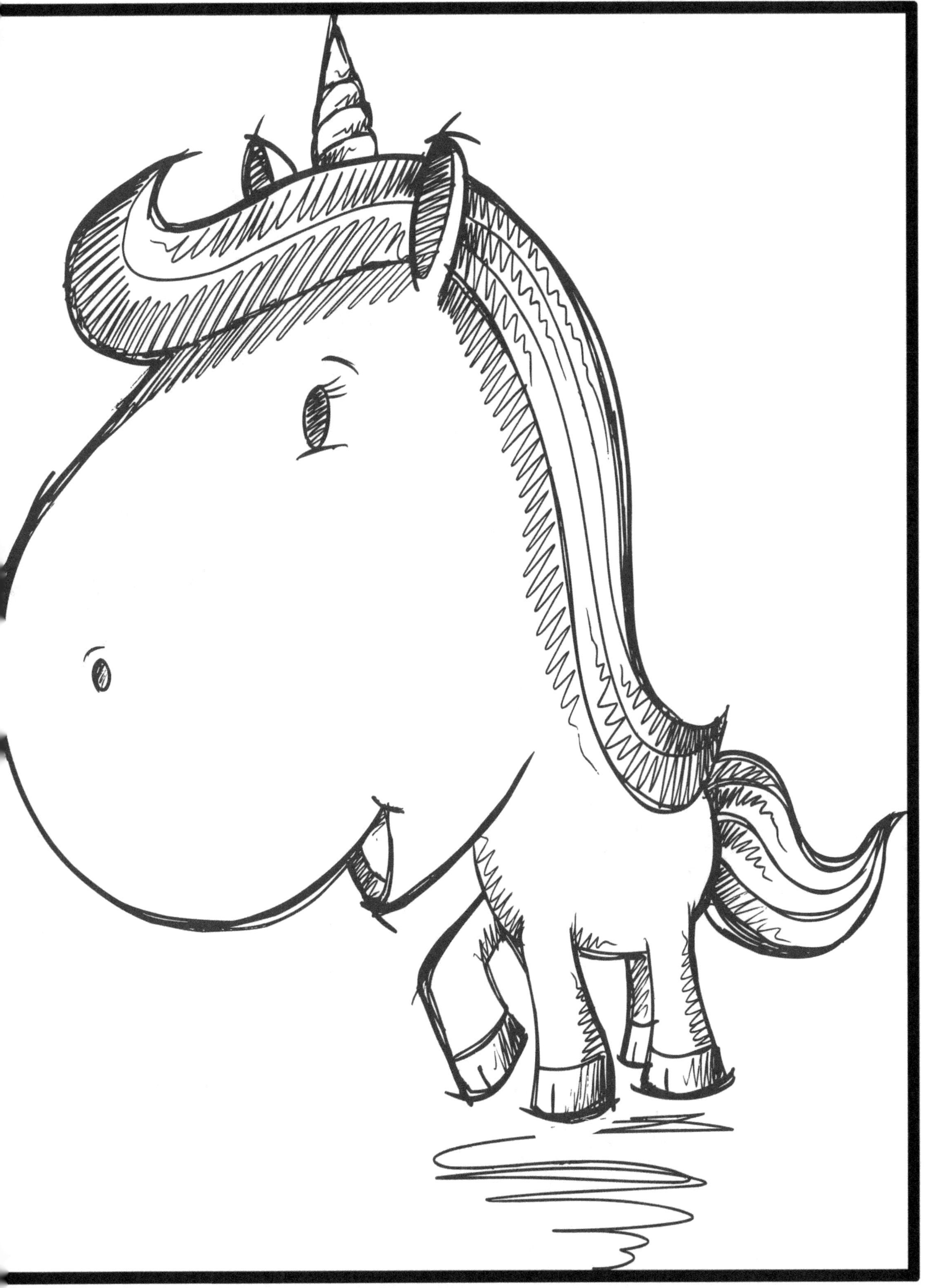

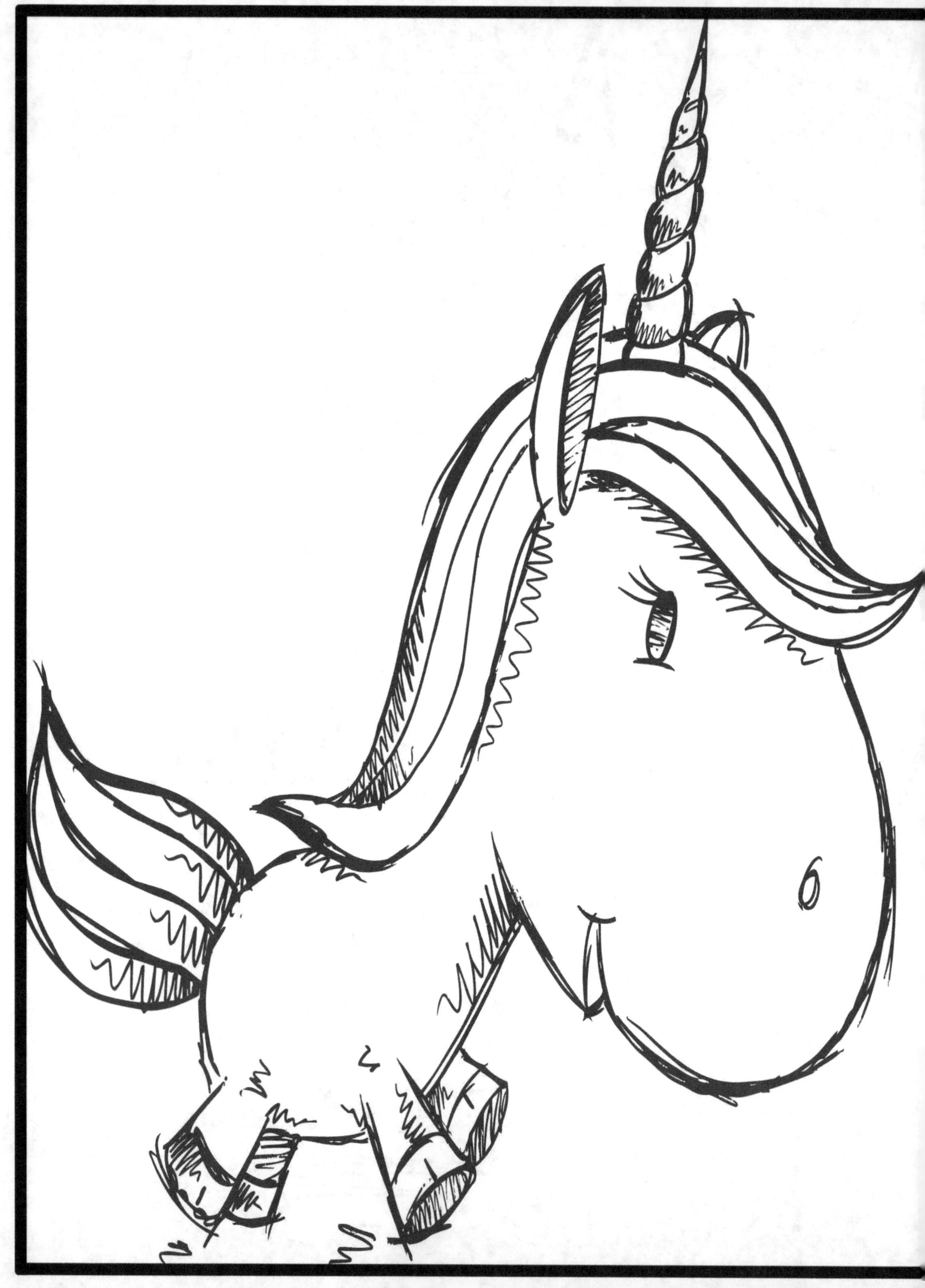

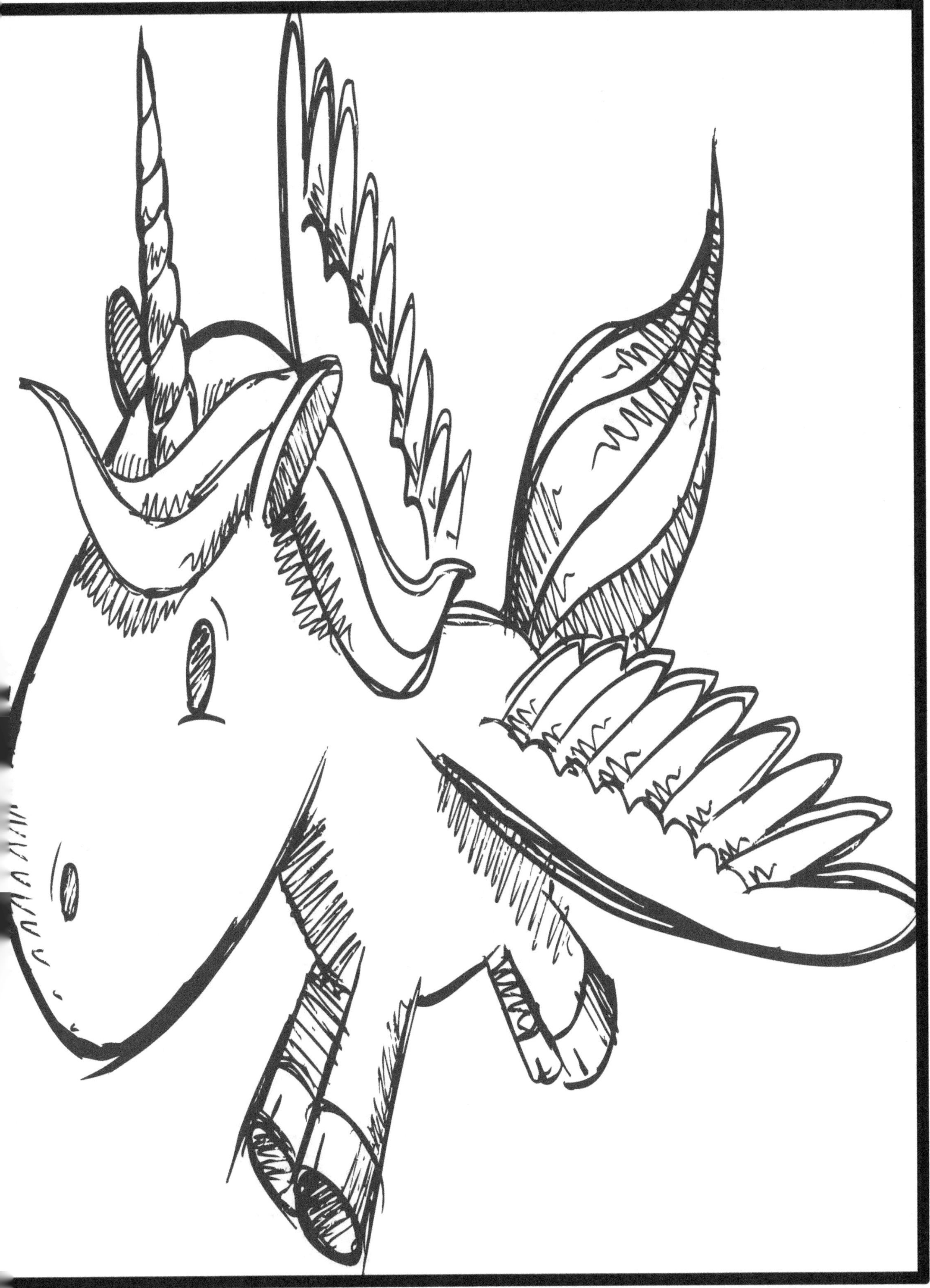

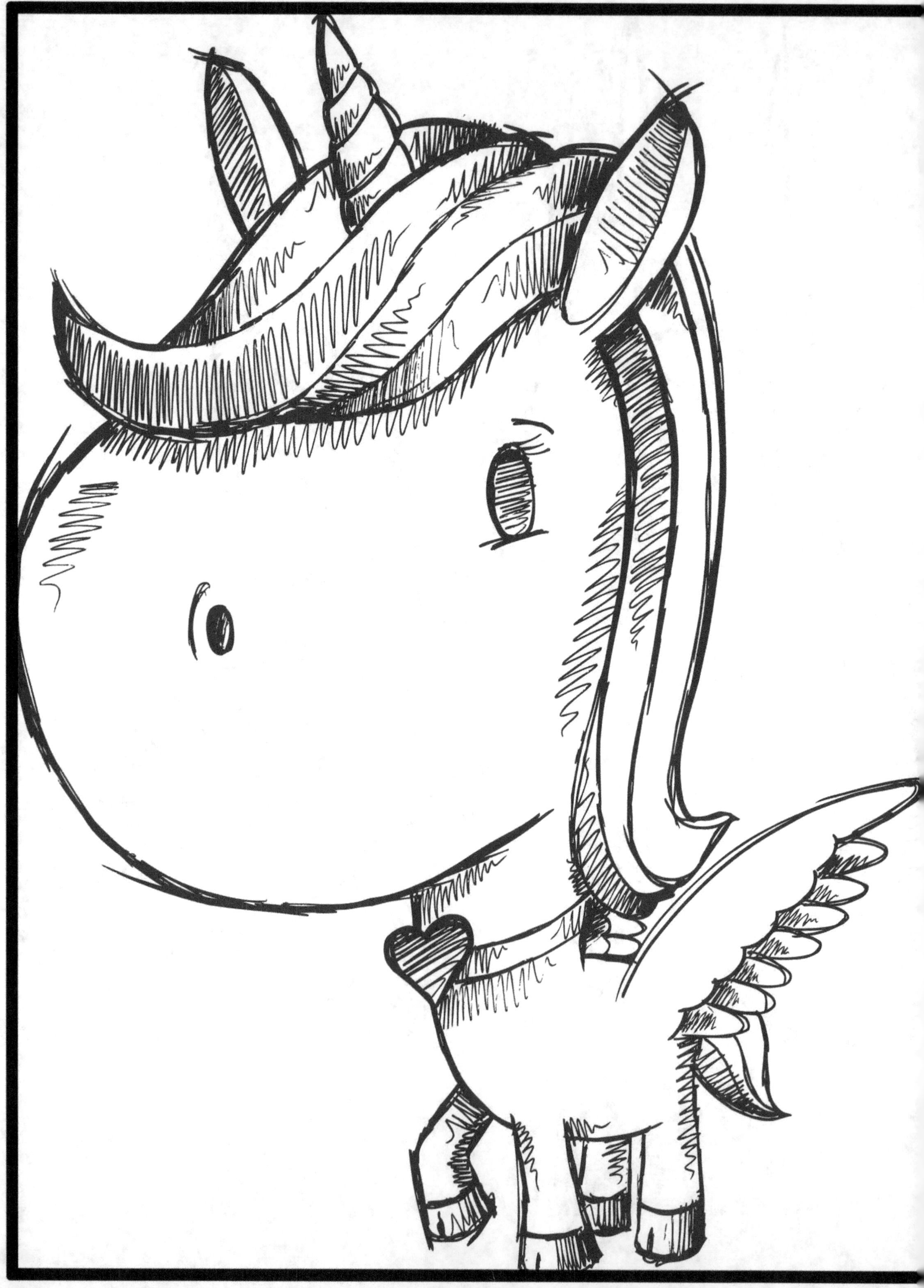

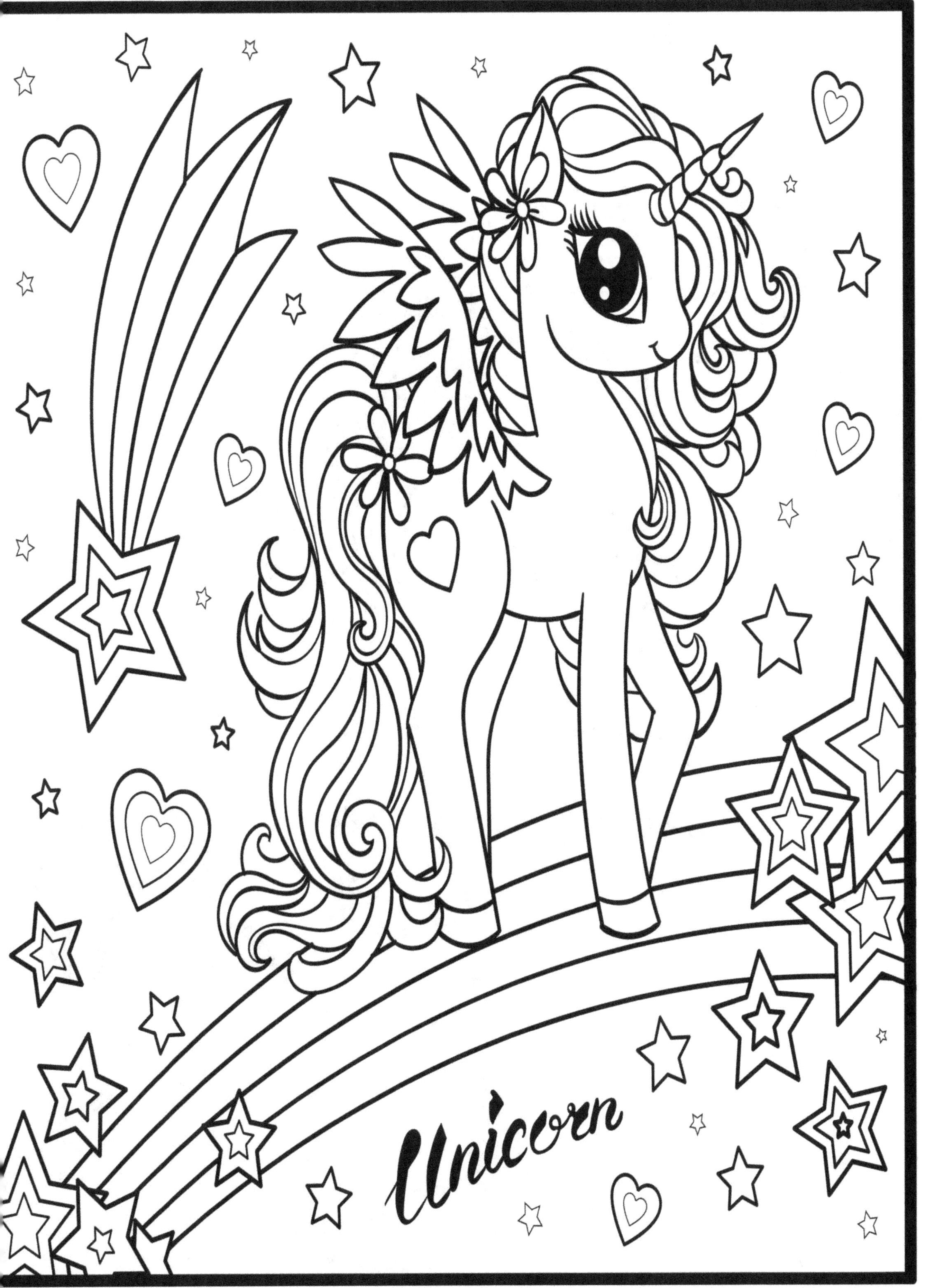
Unicorn

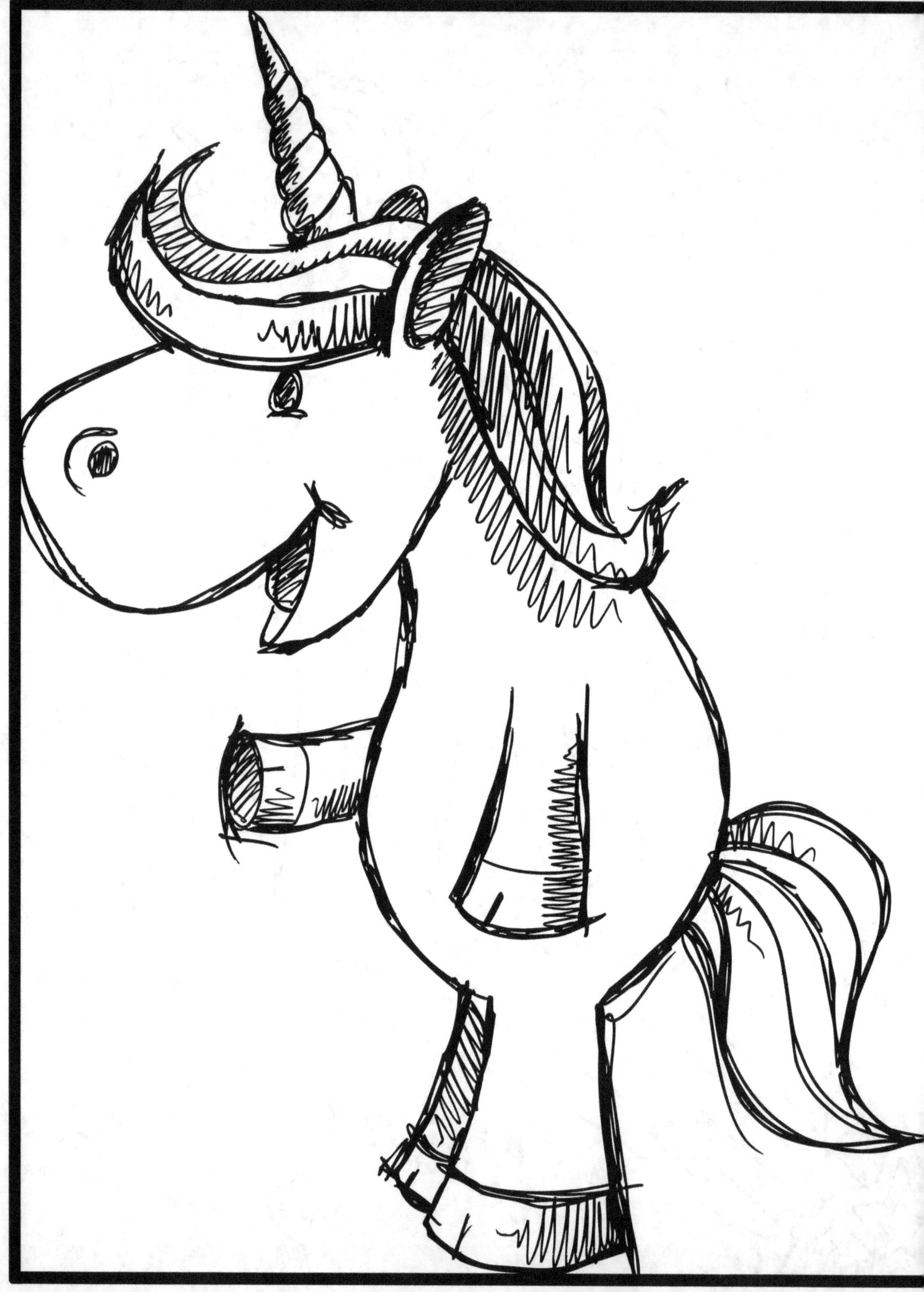

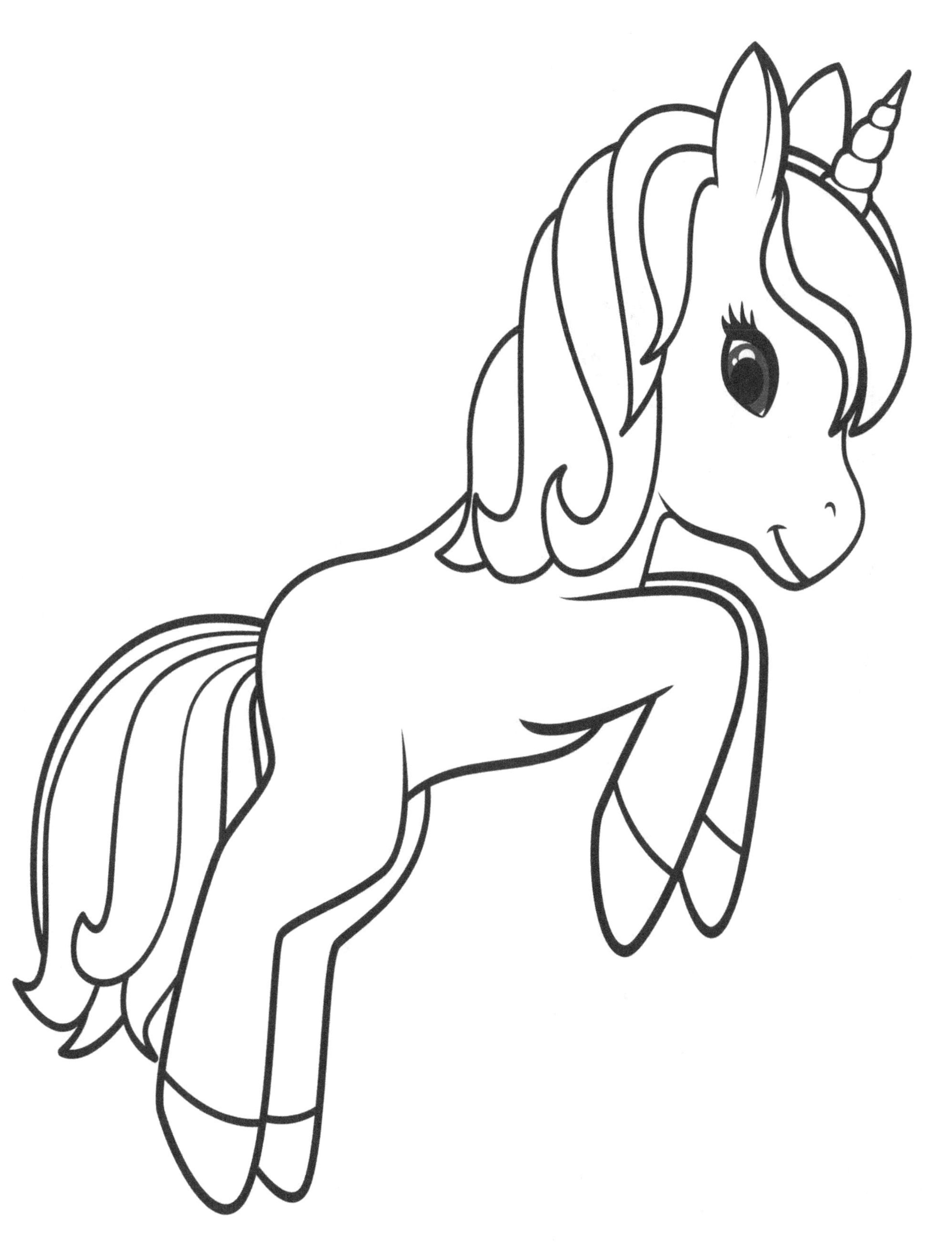

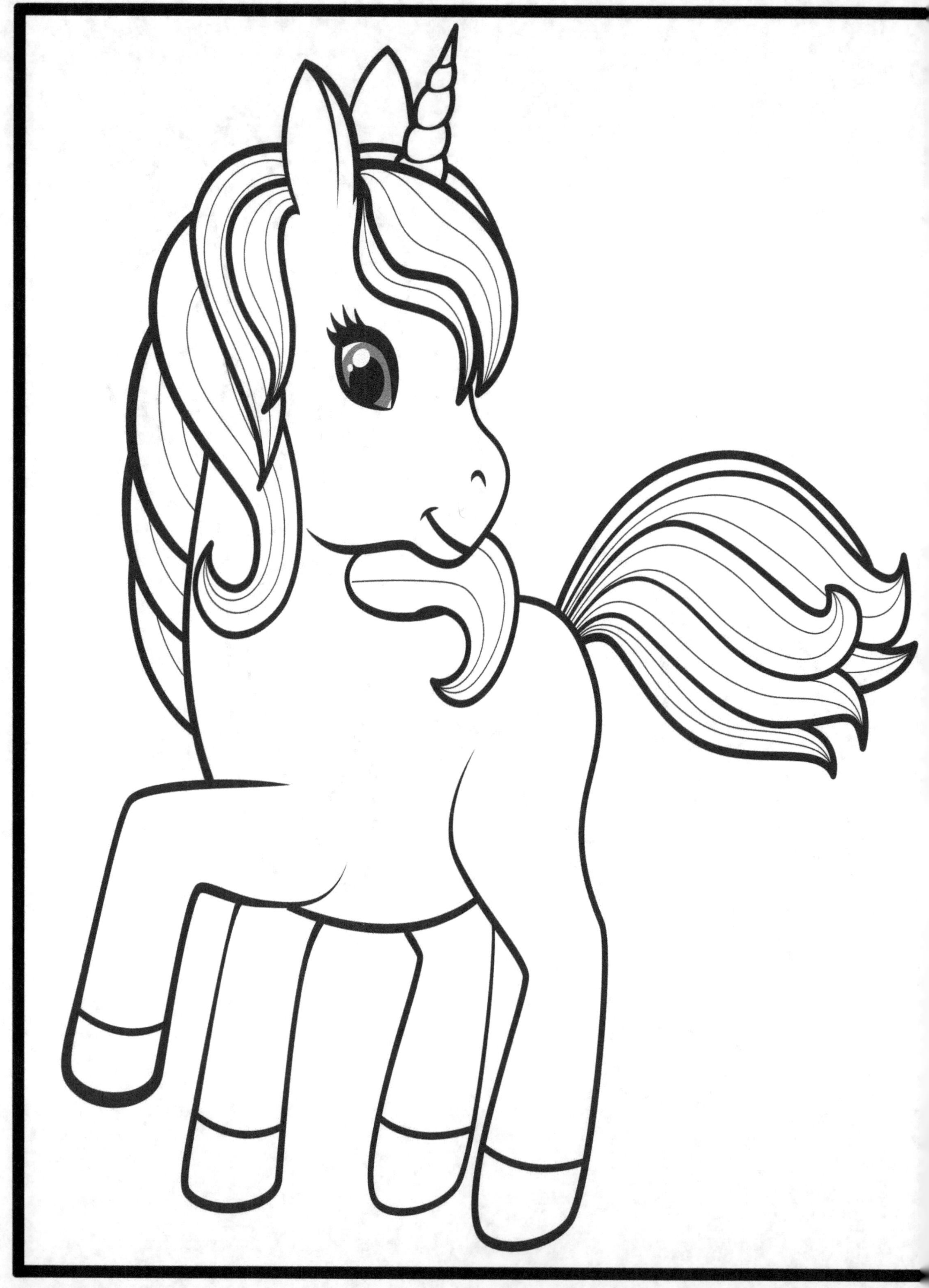

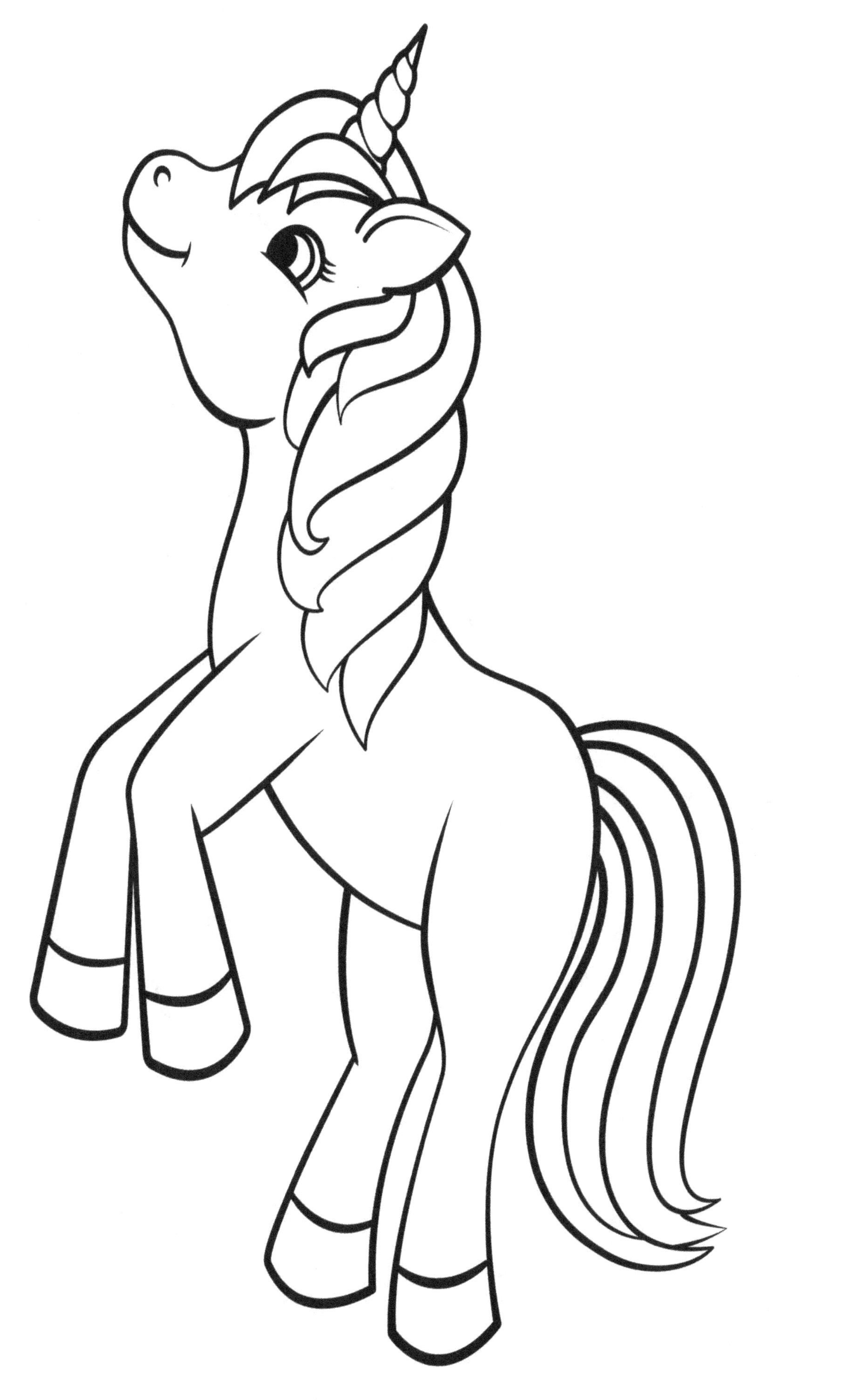

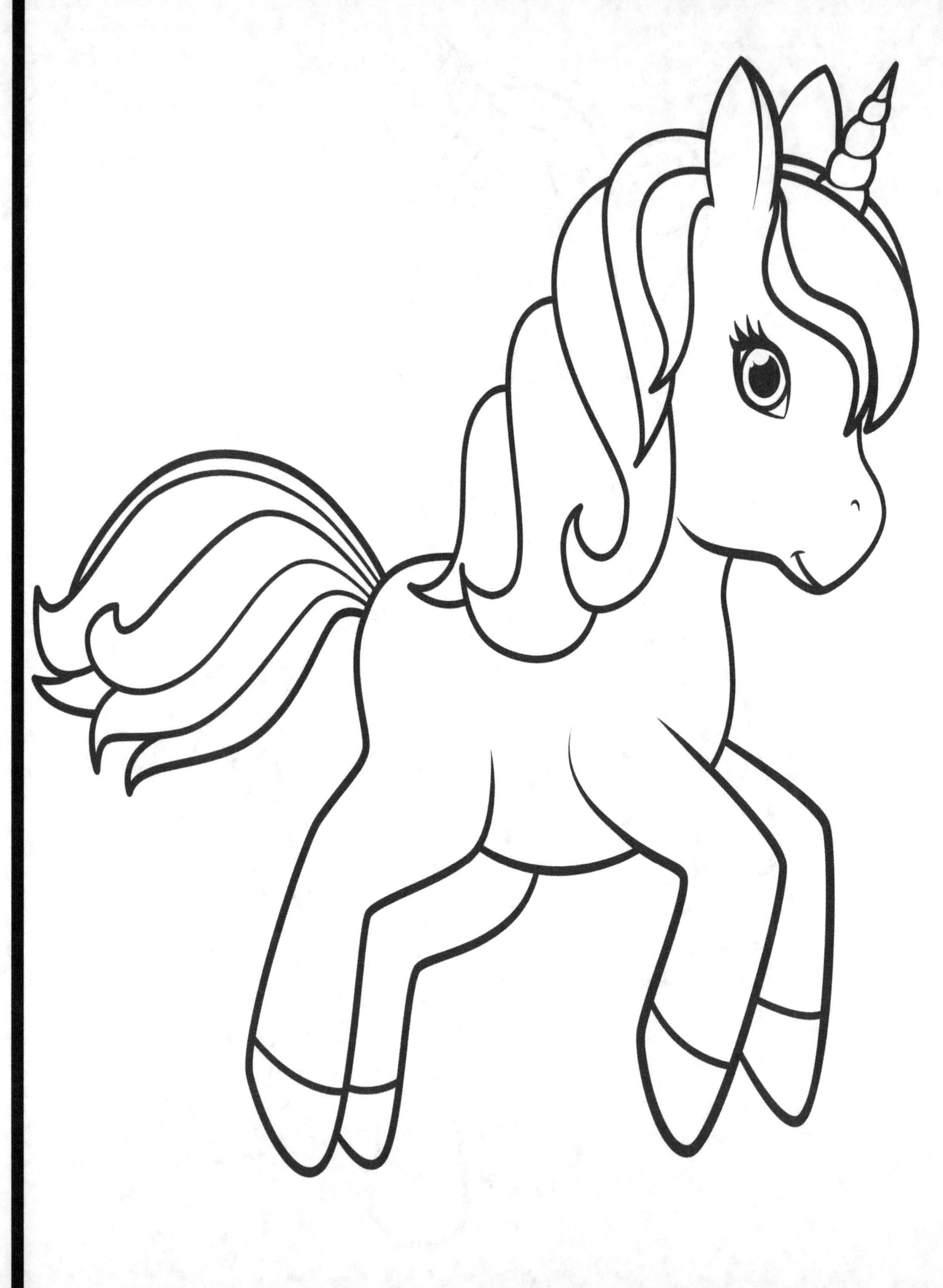

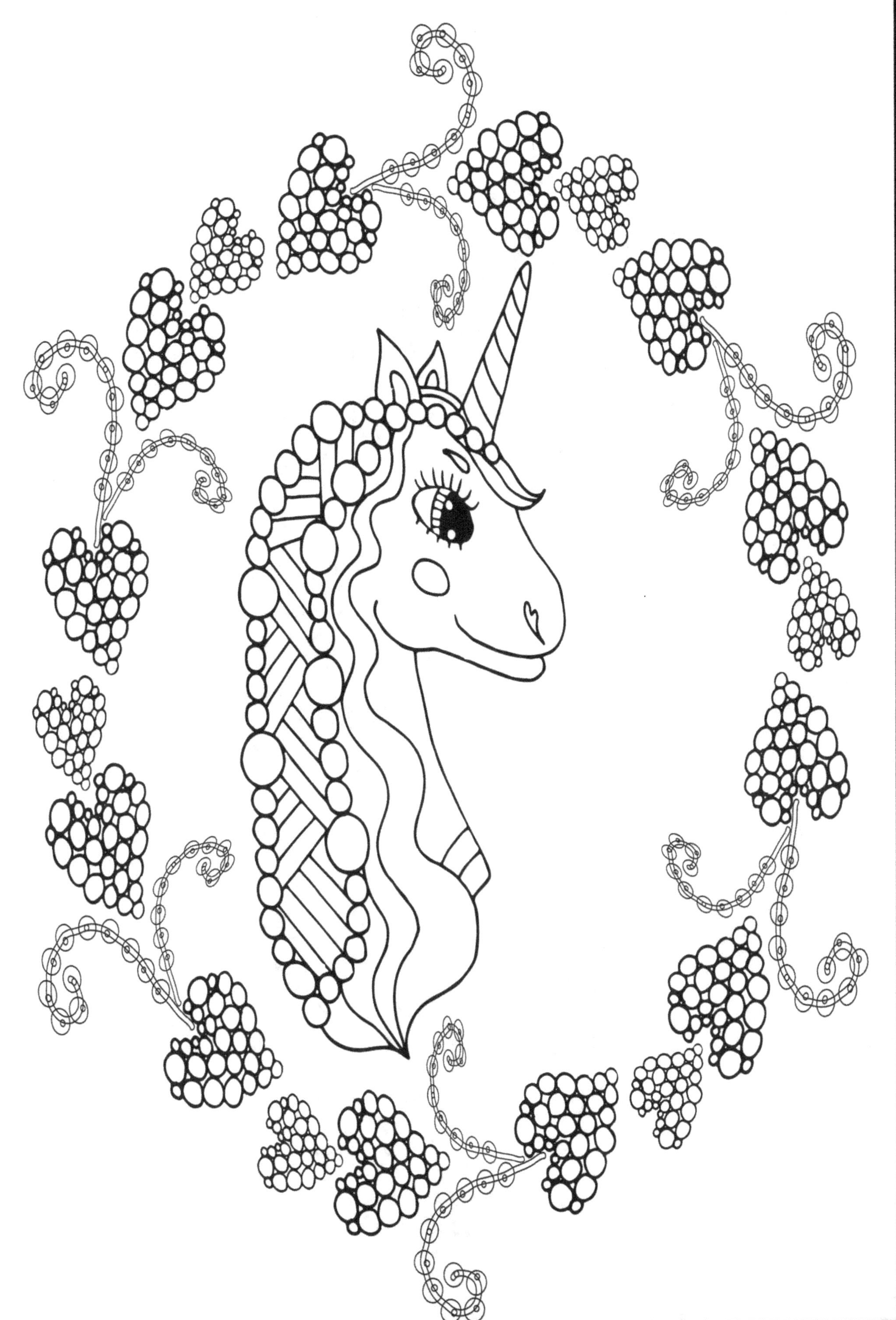

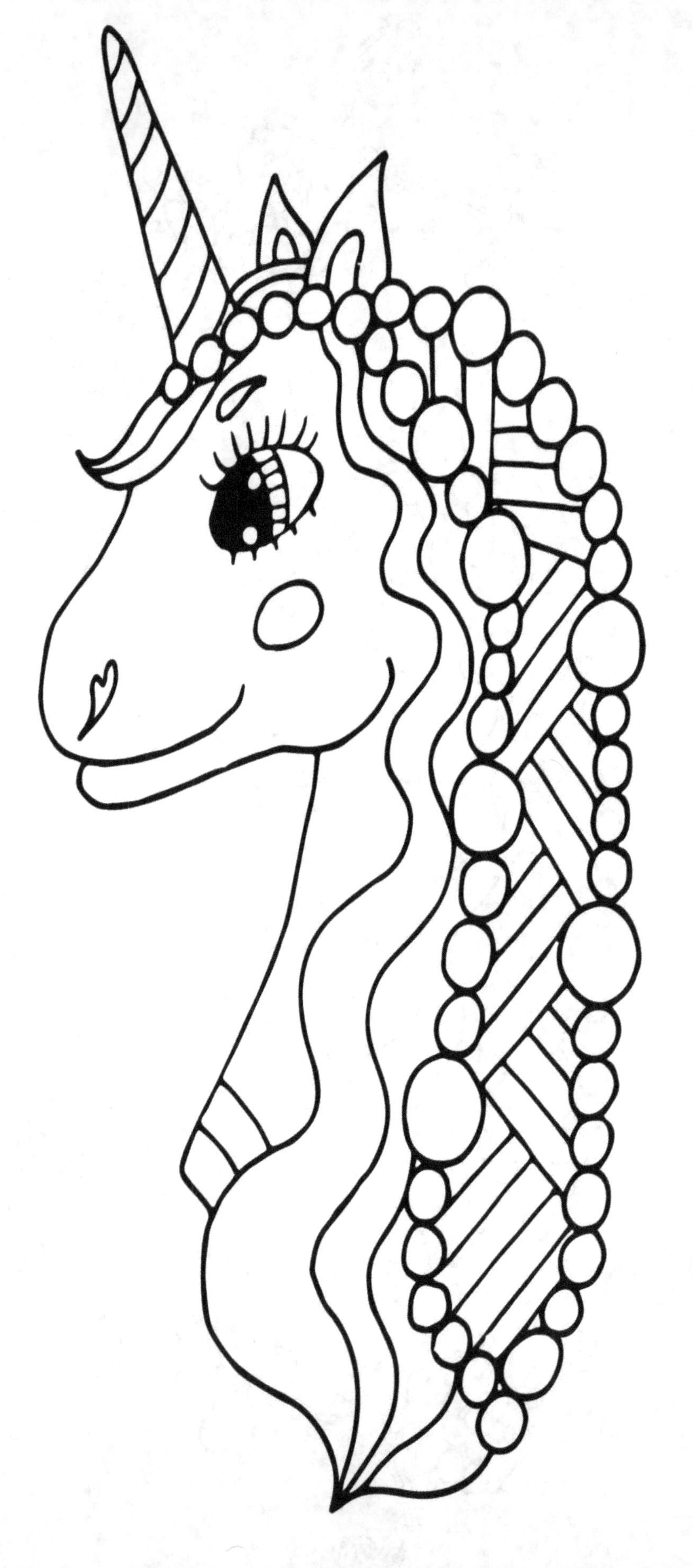

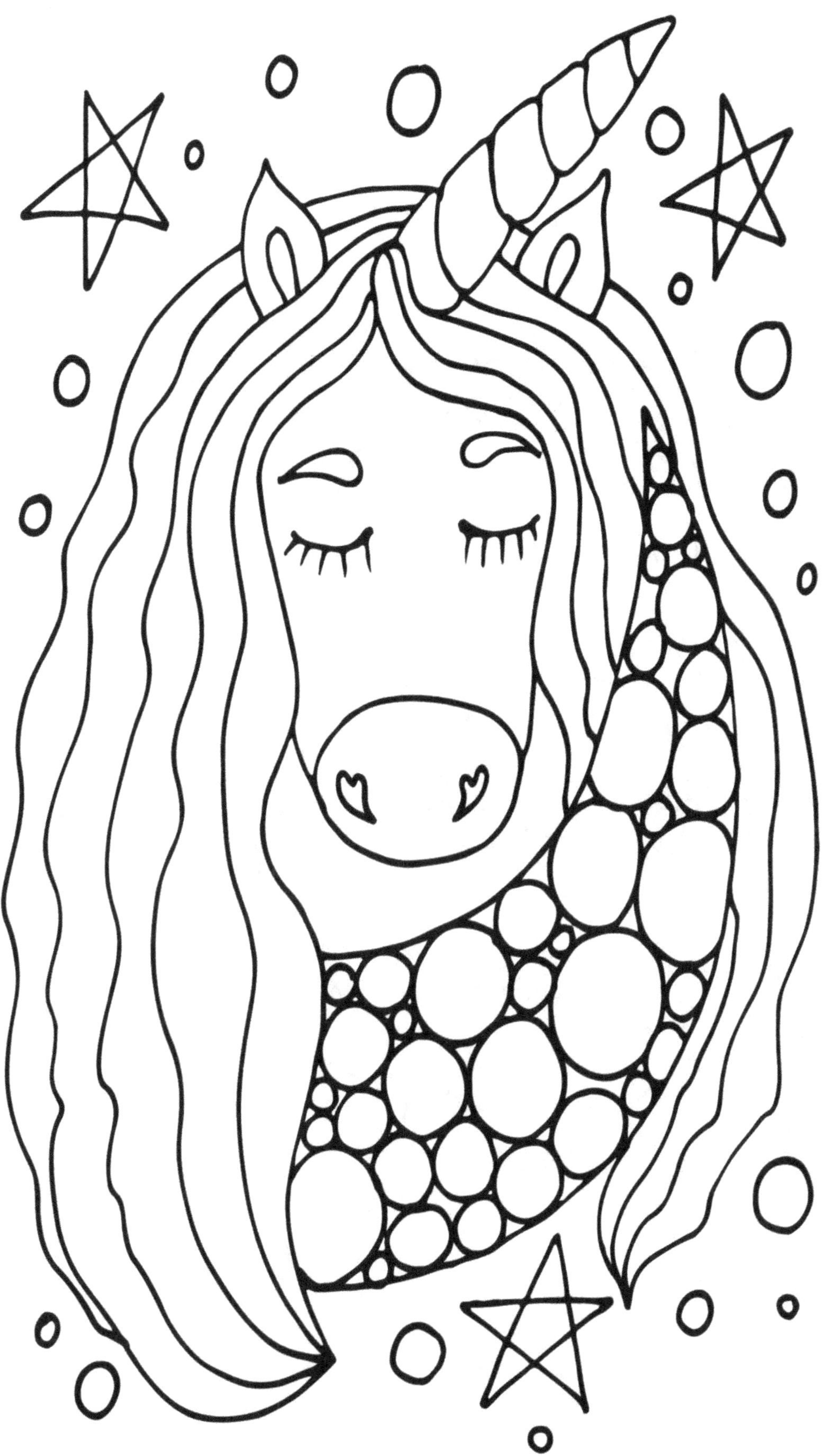

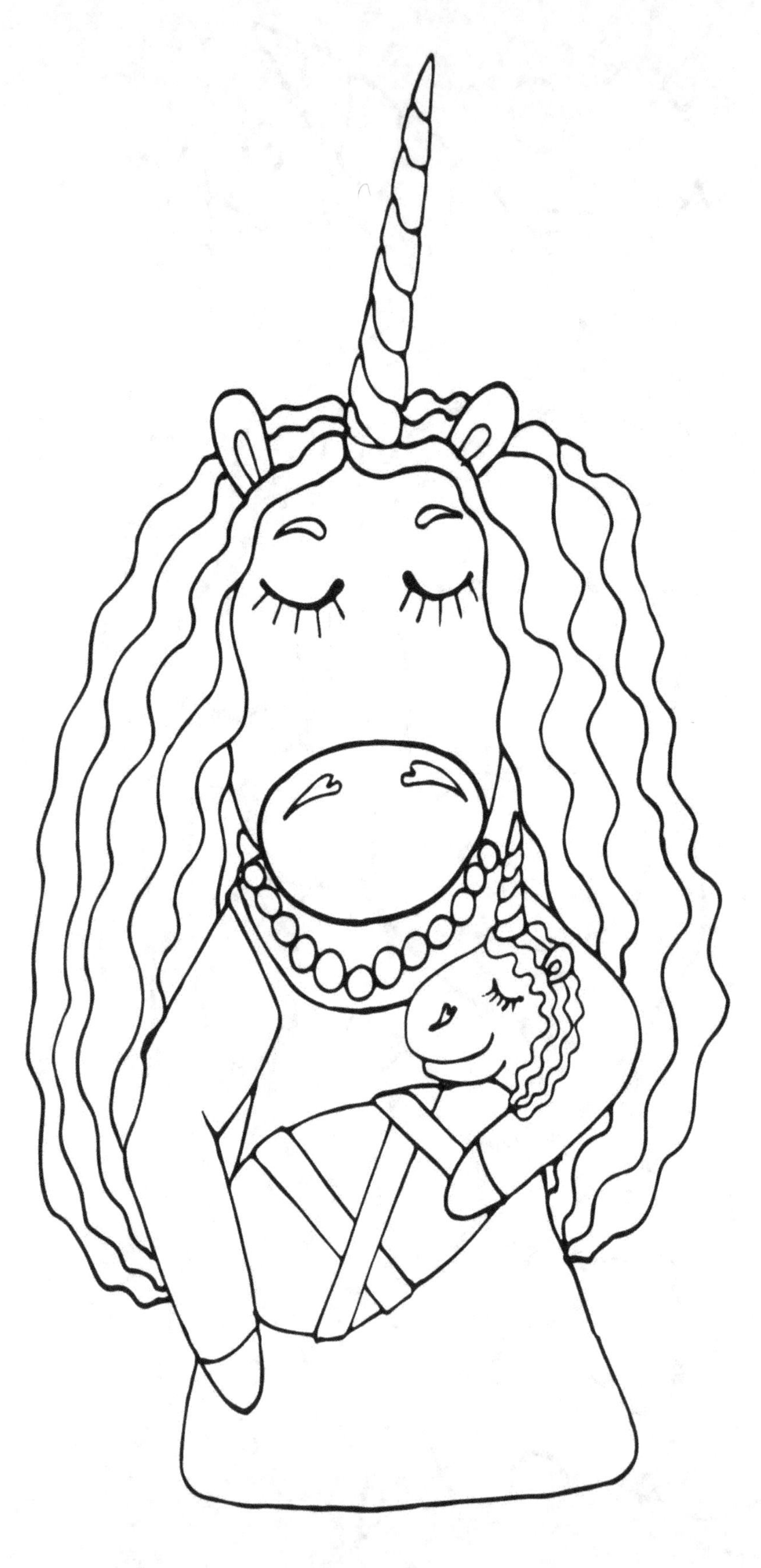

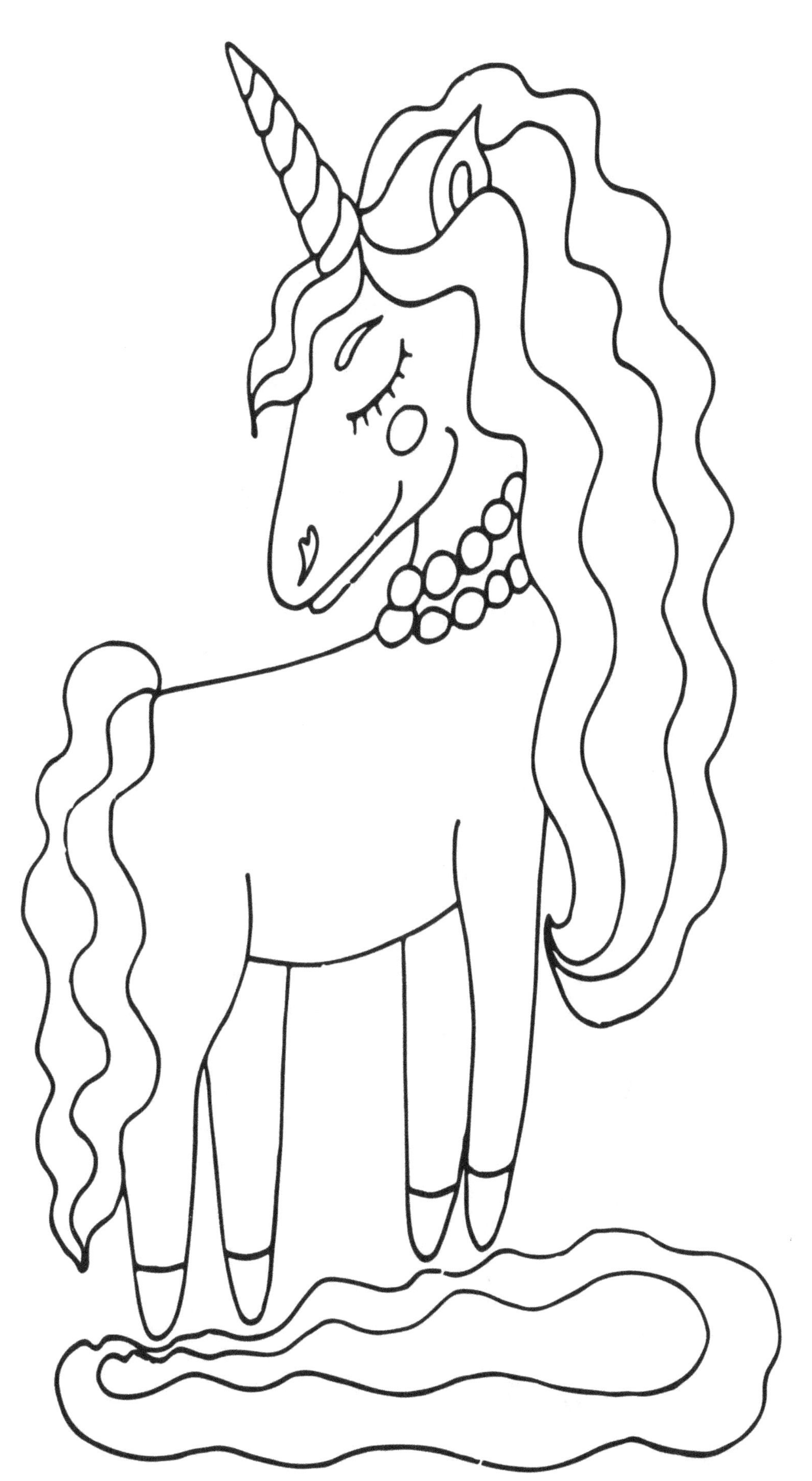

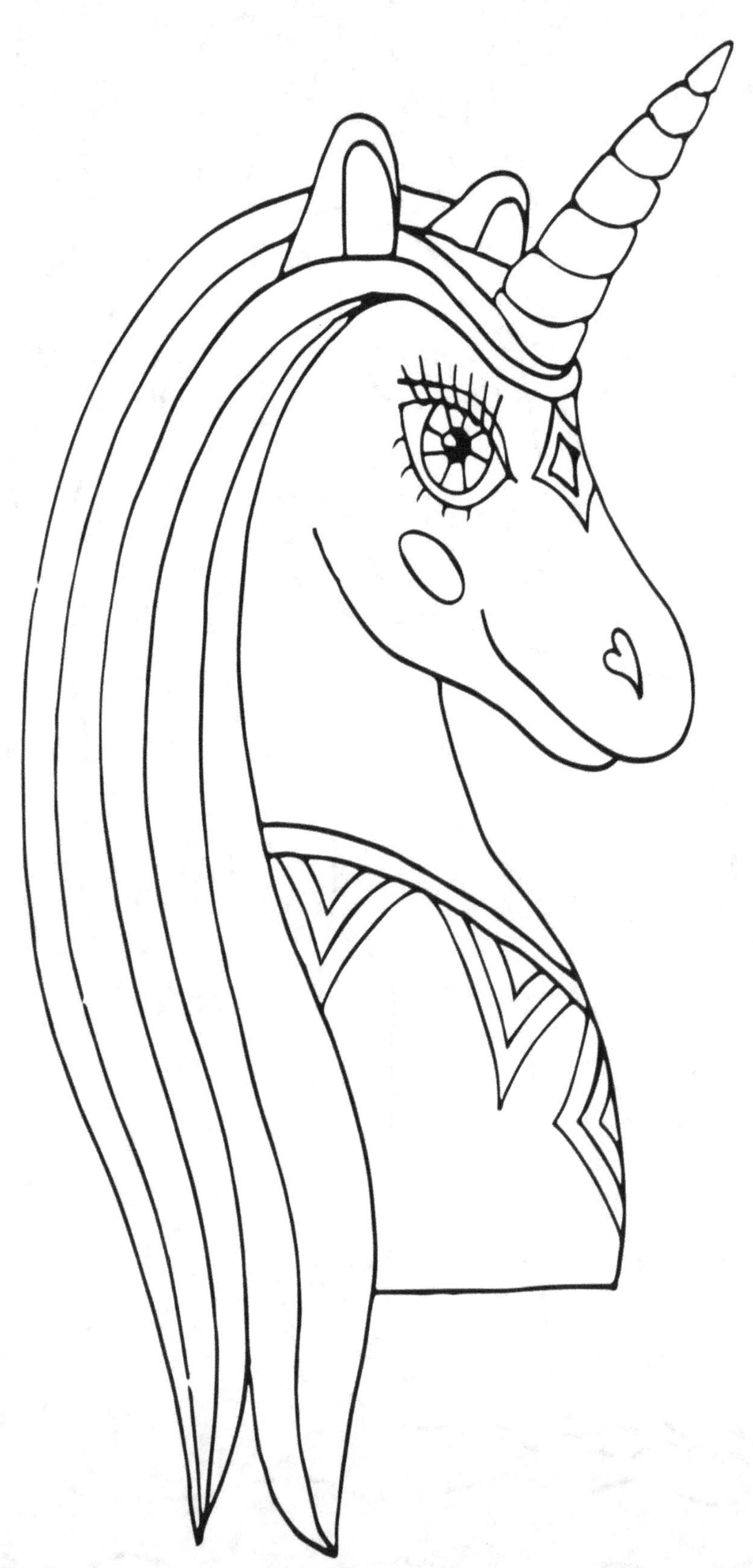

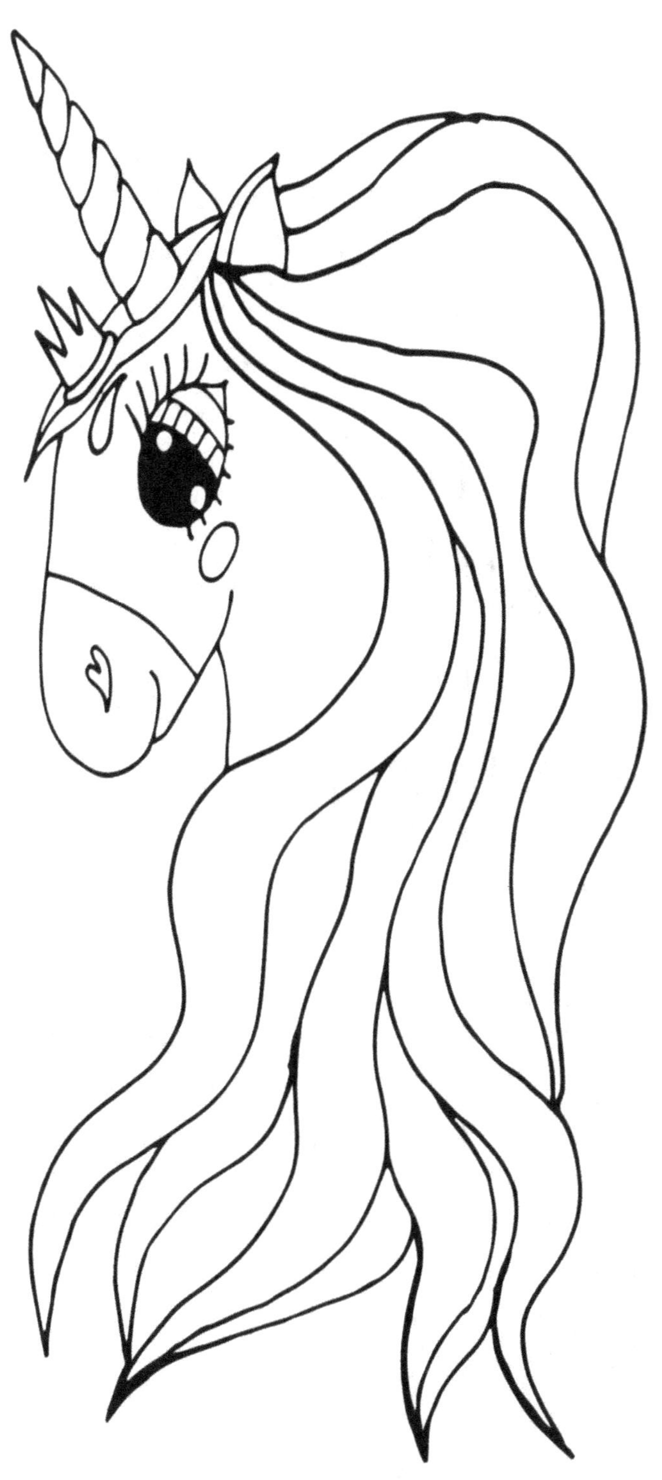

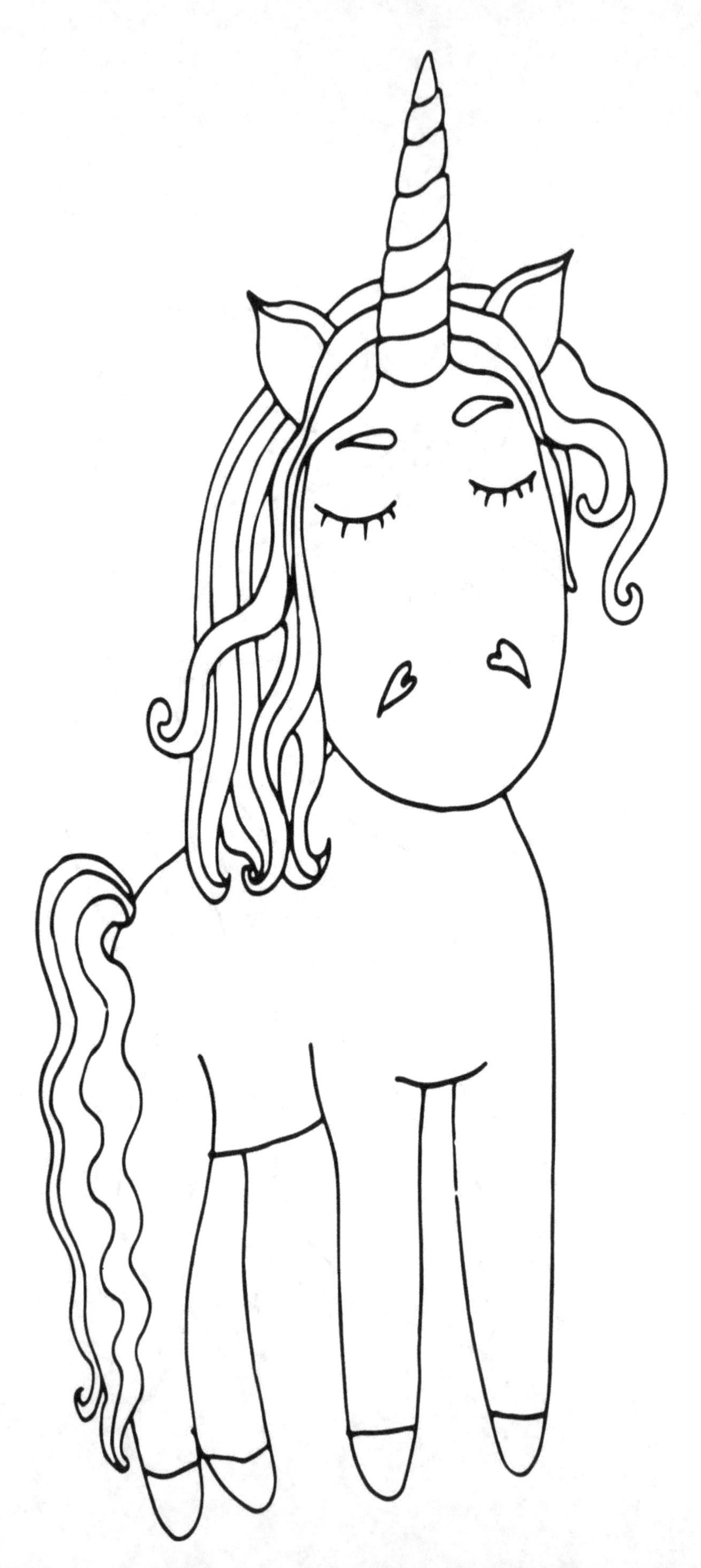

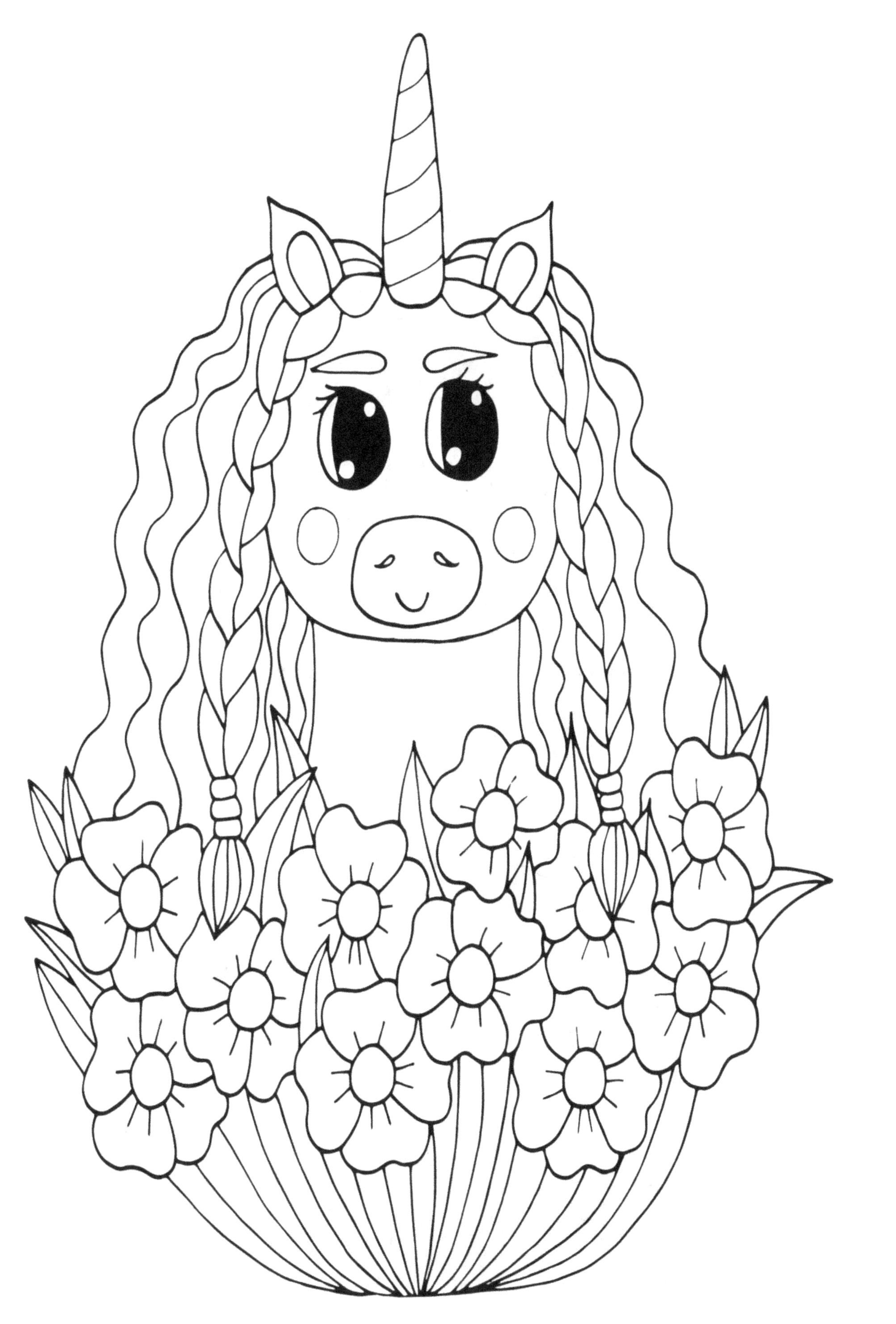

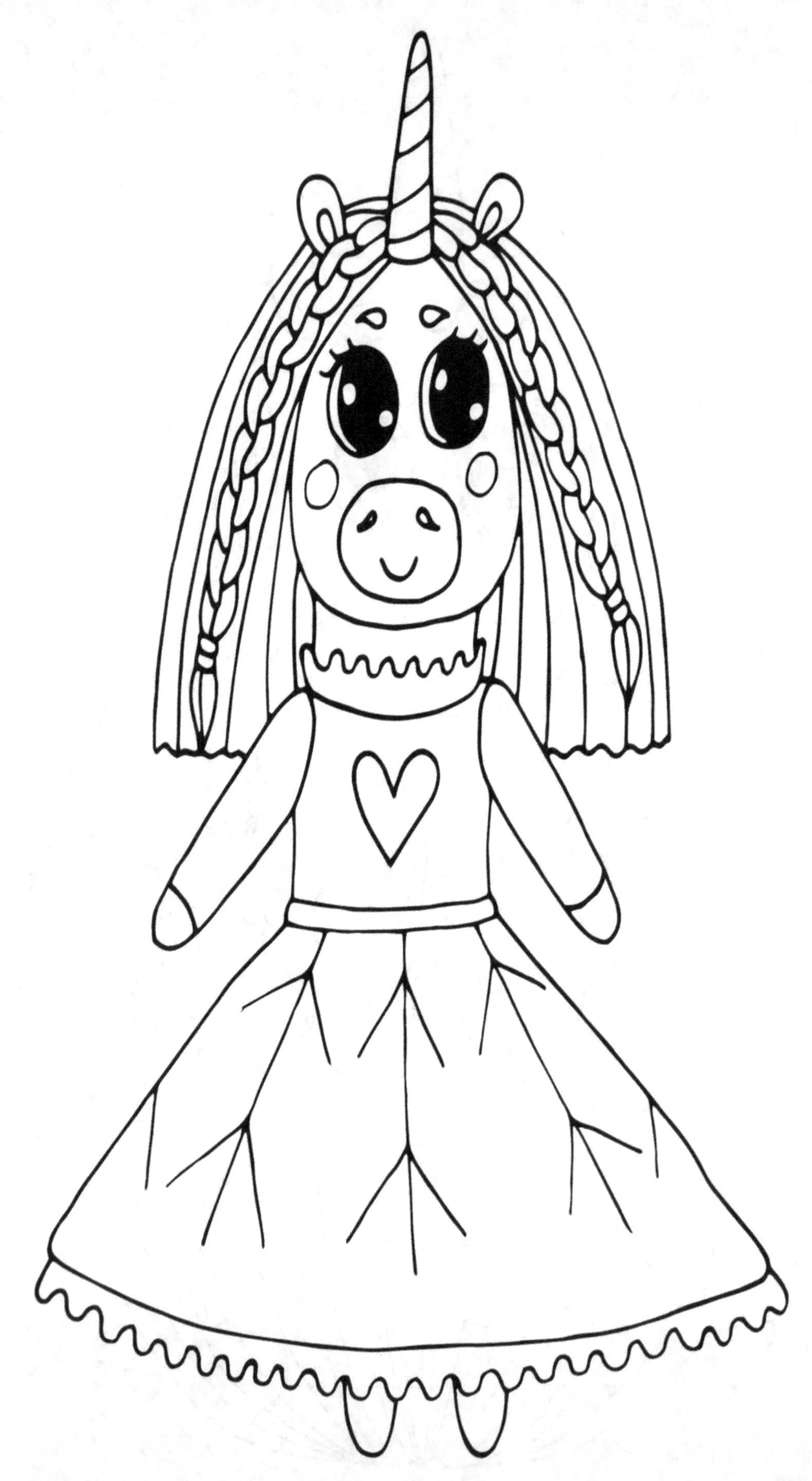

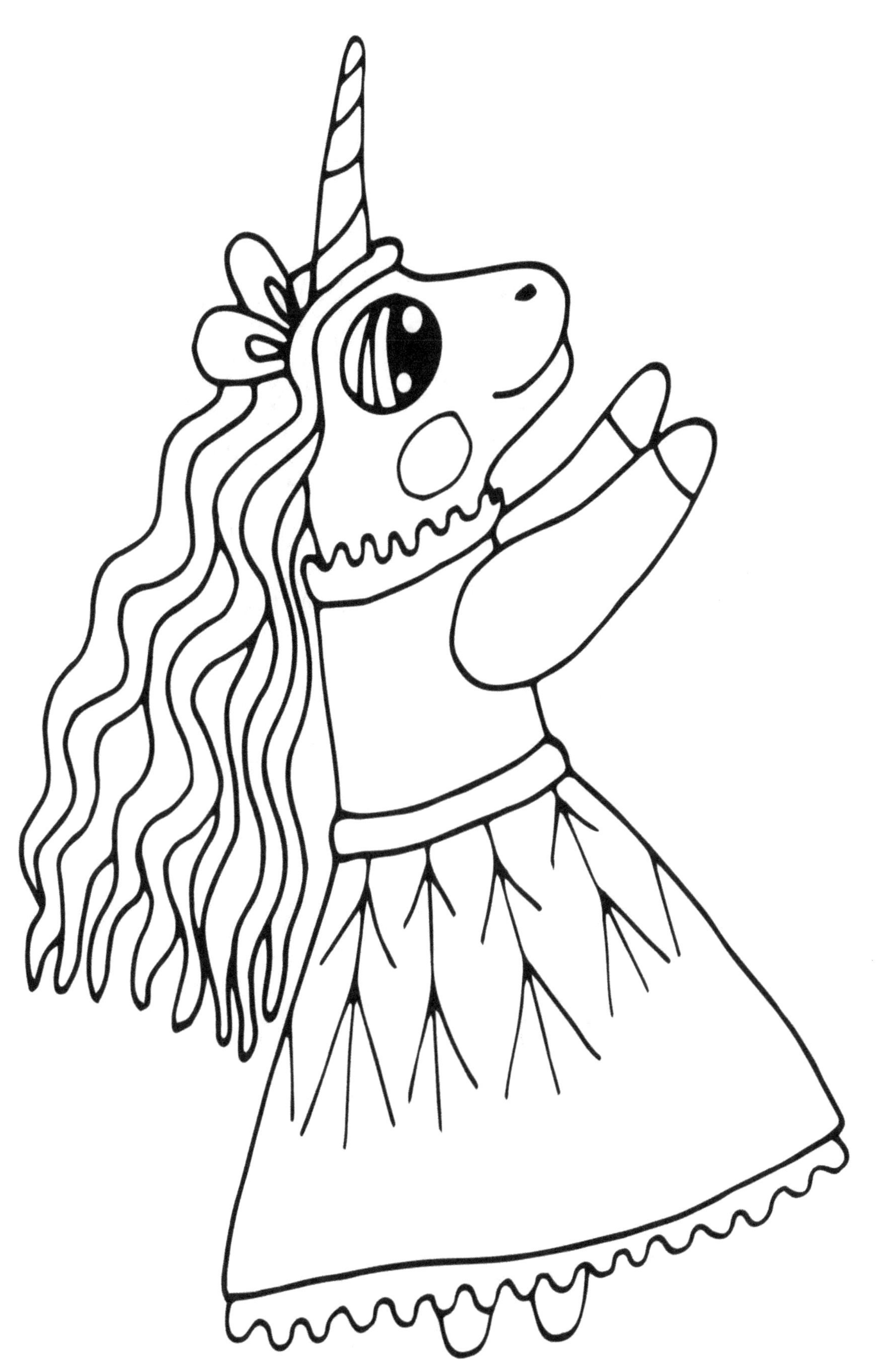

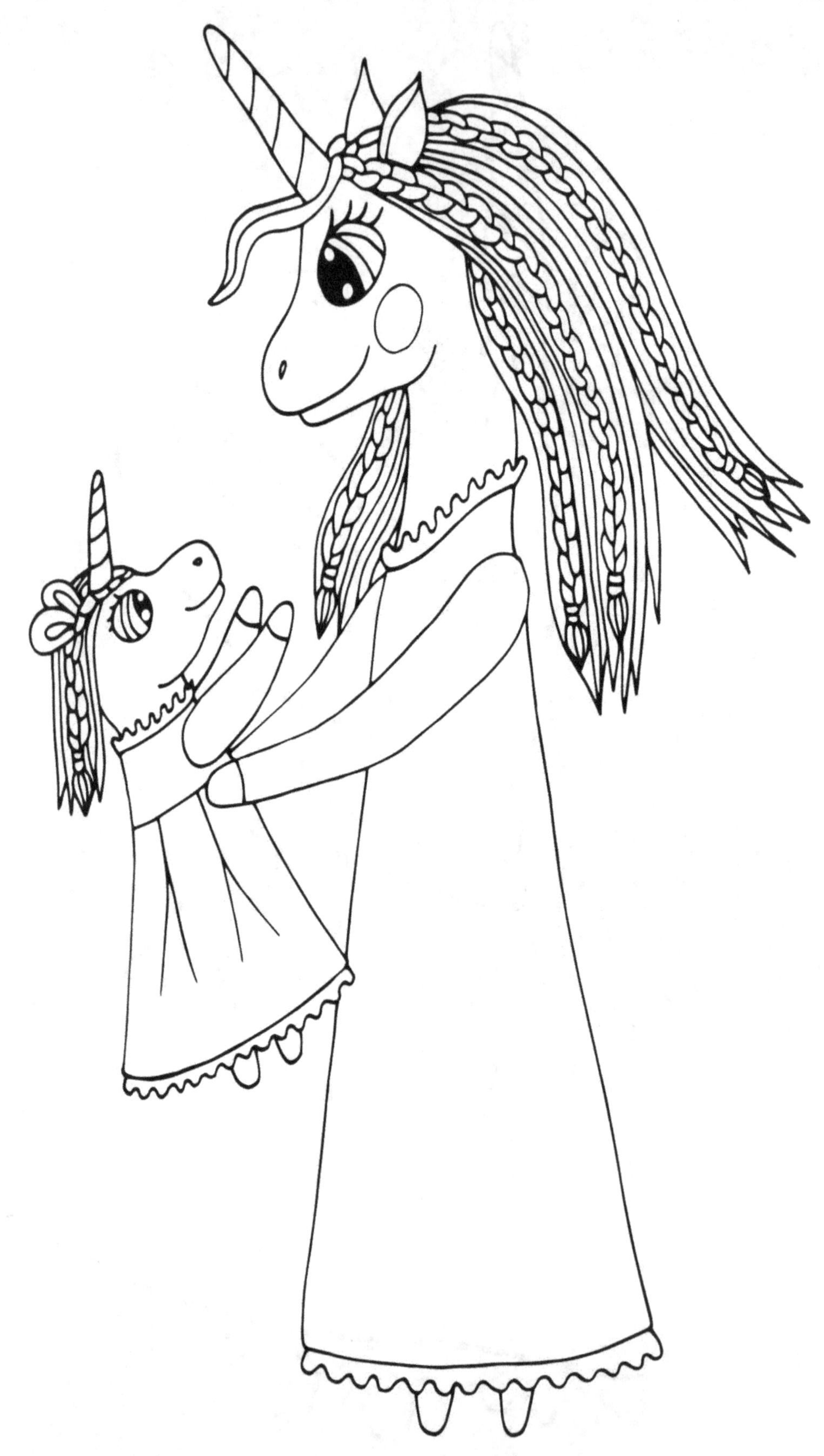

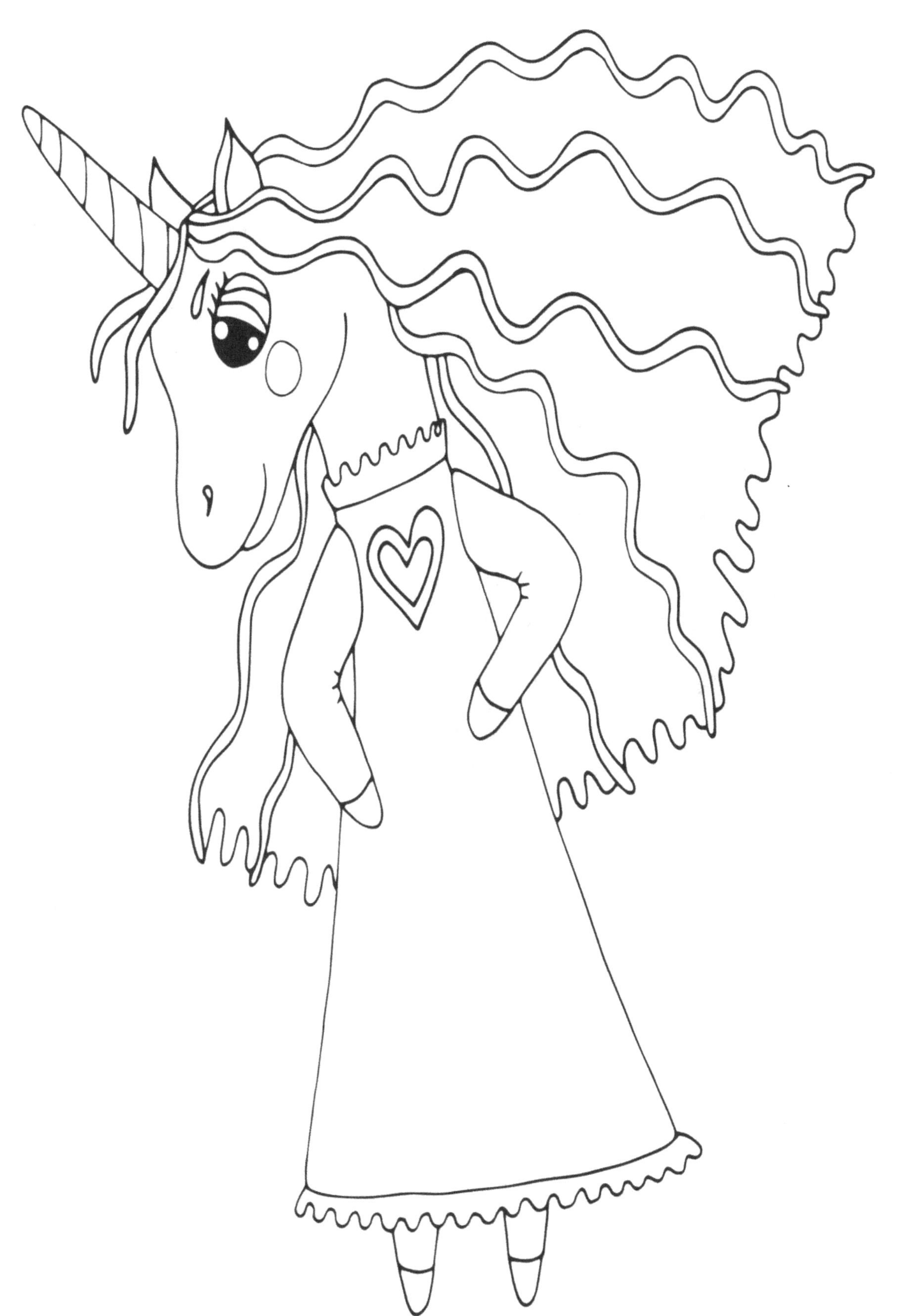

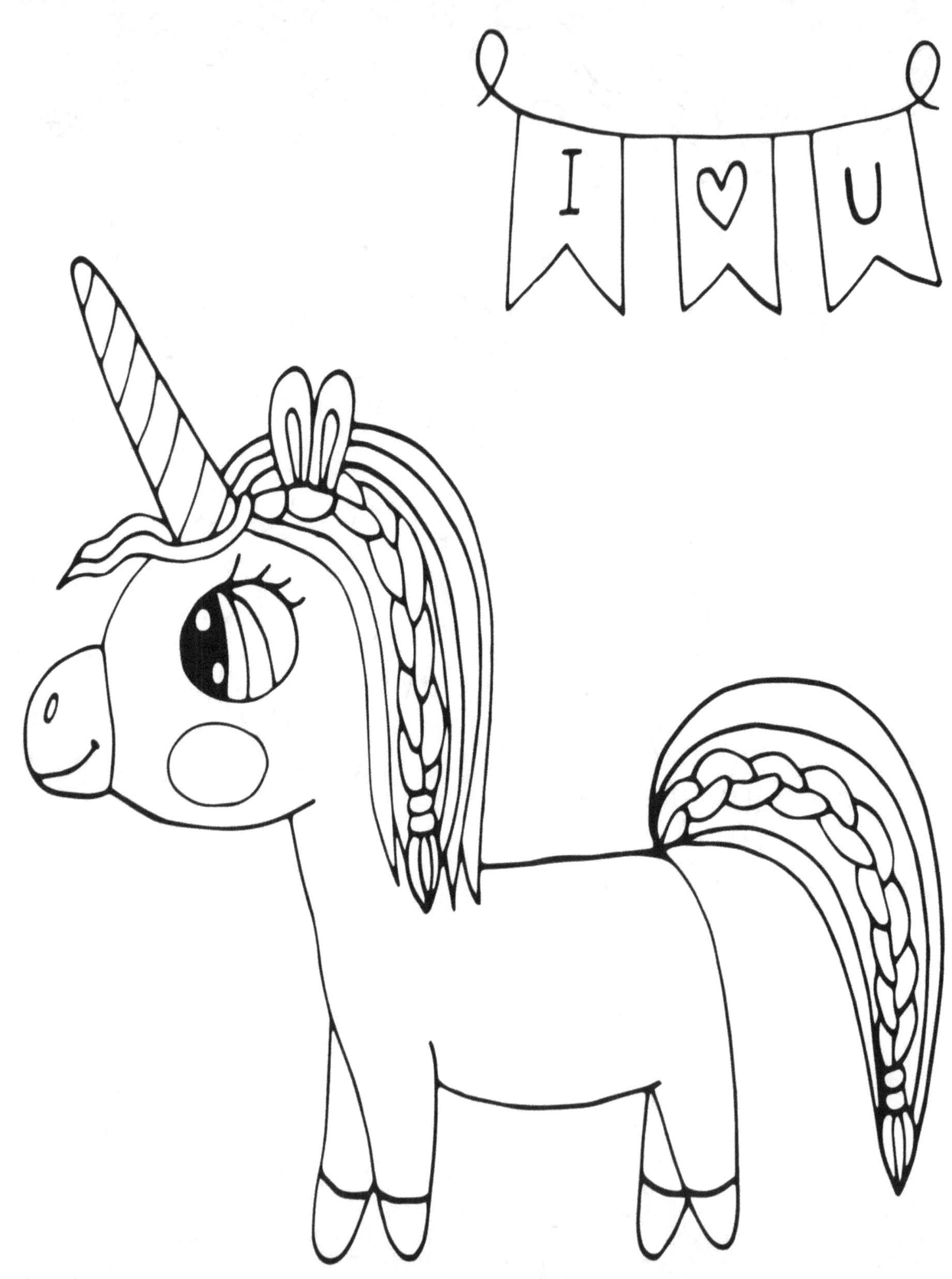

I
U

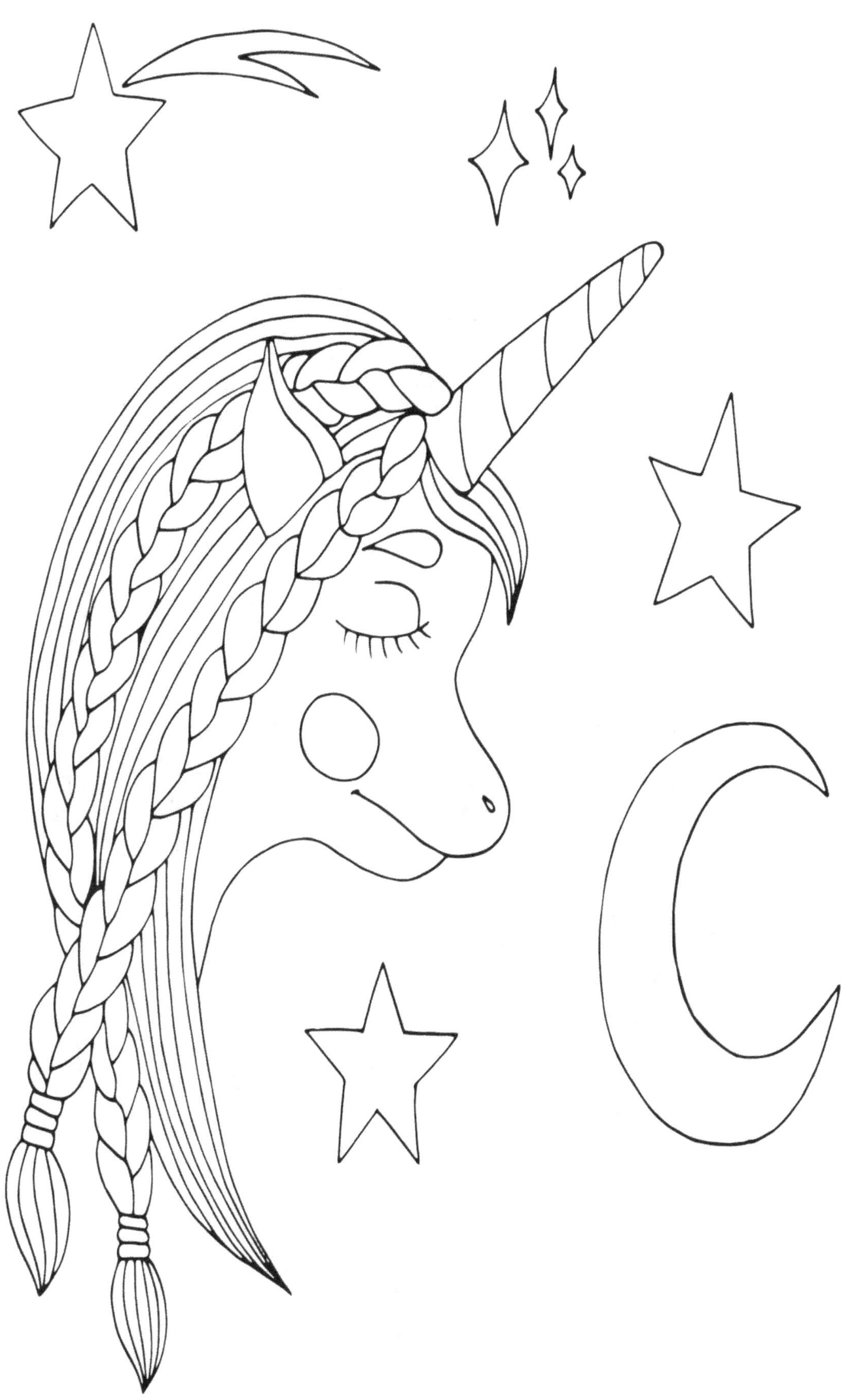

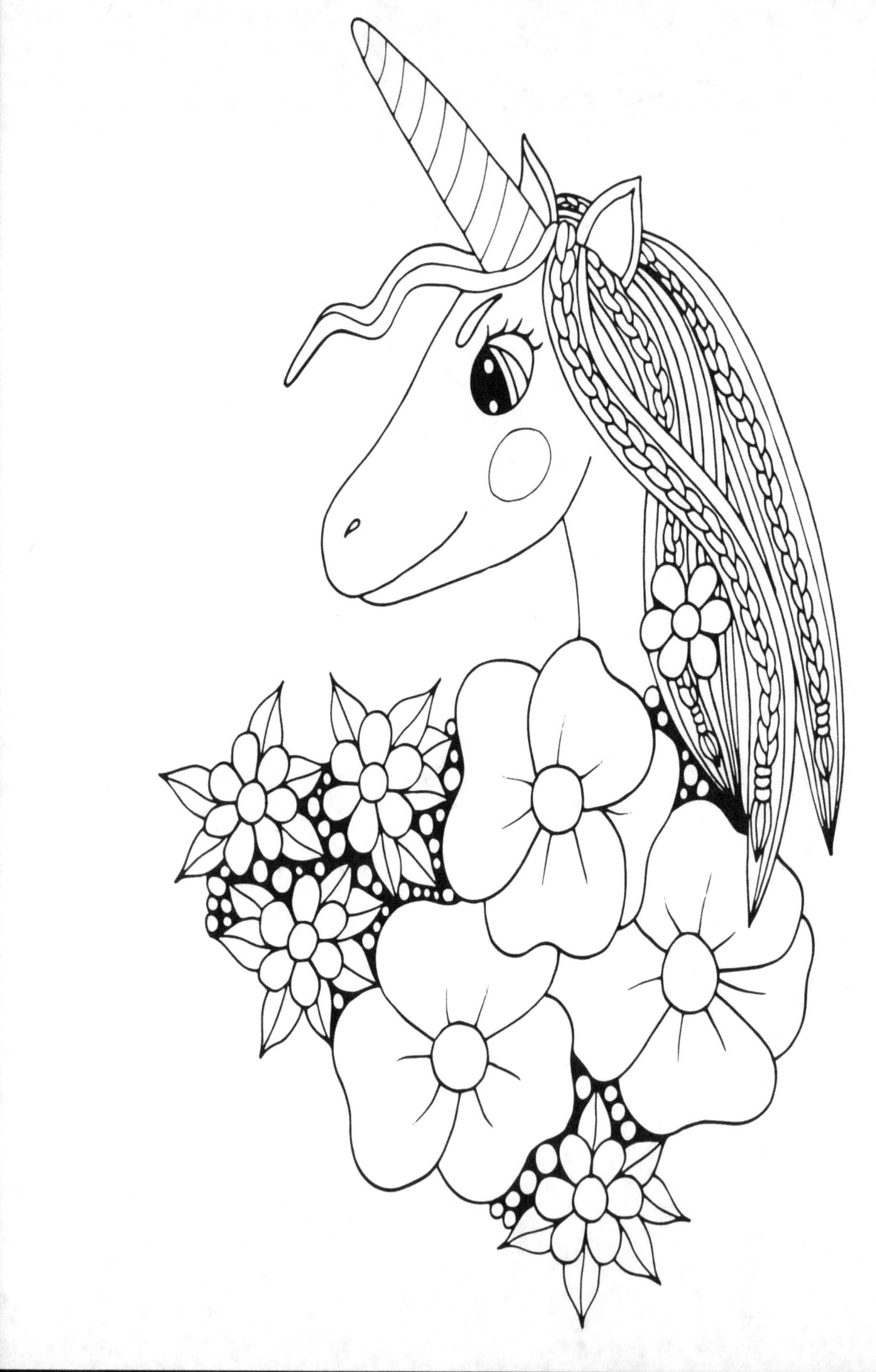

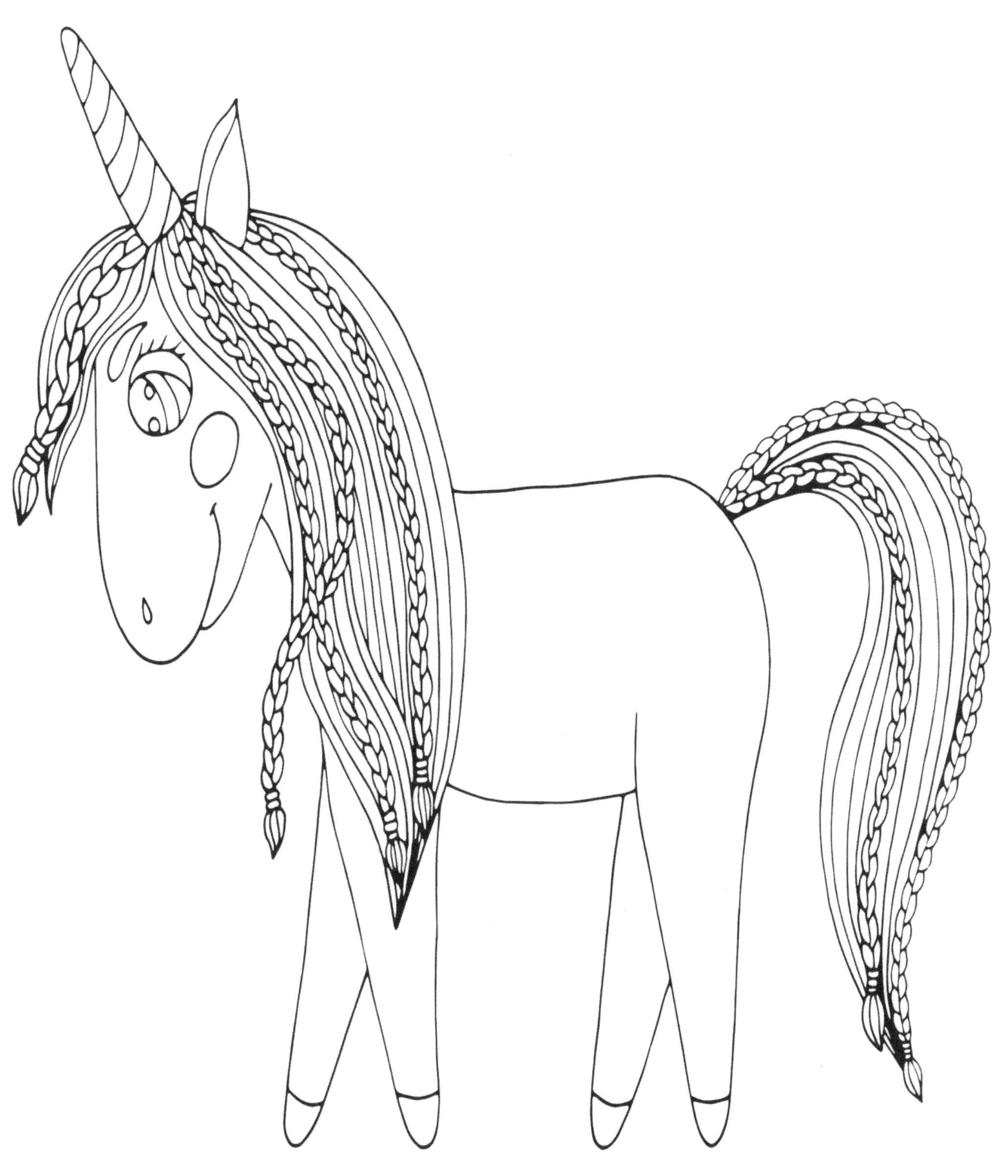

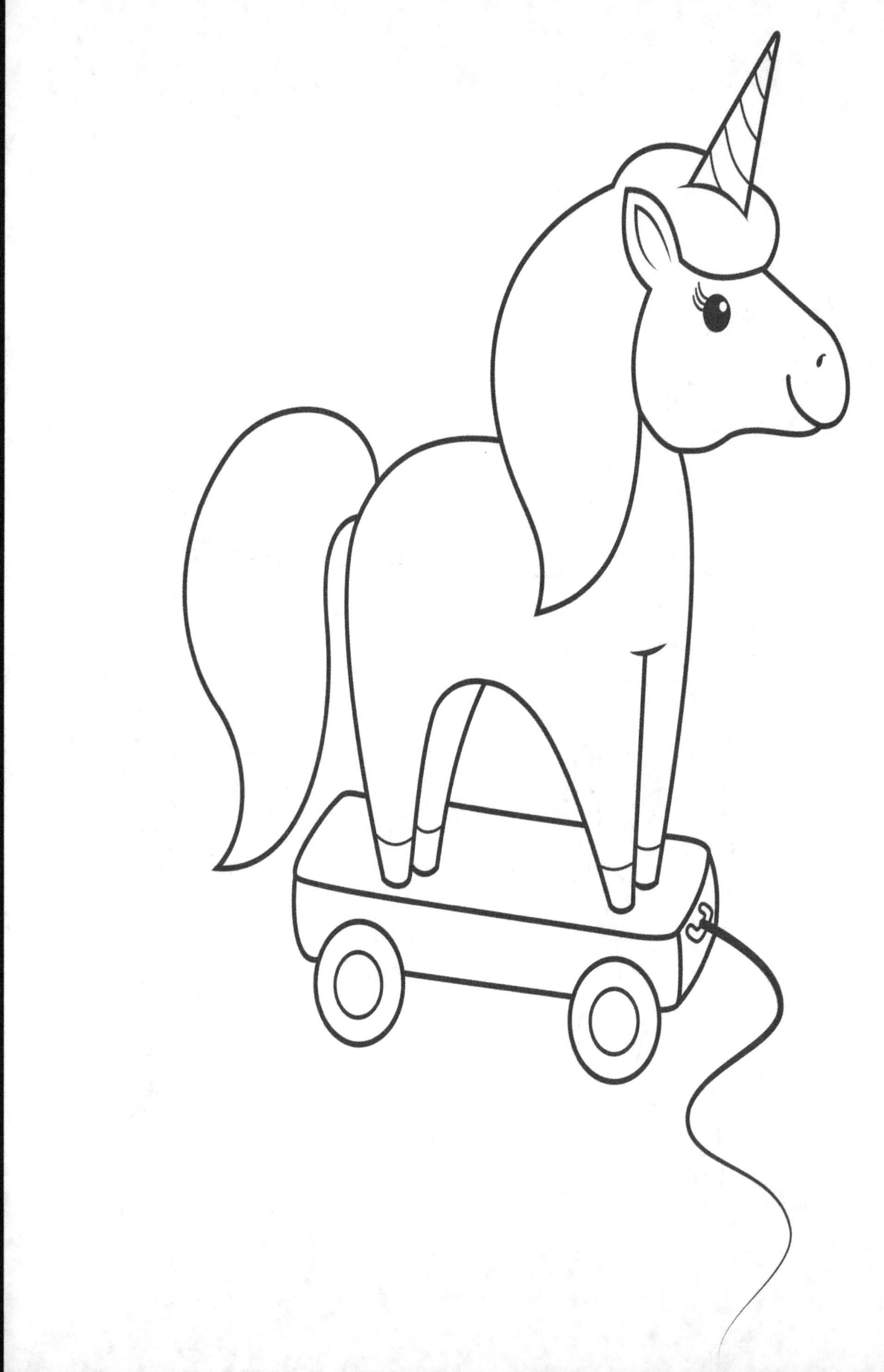

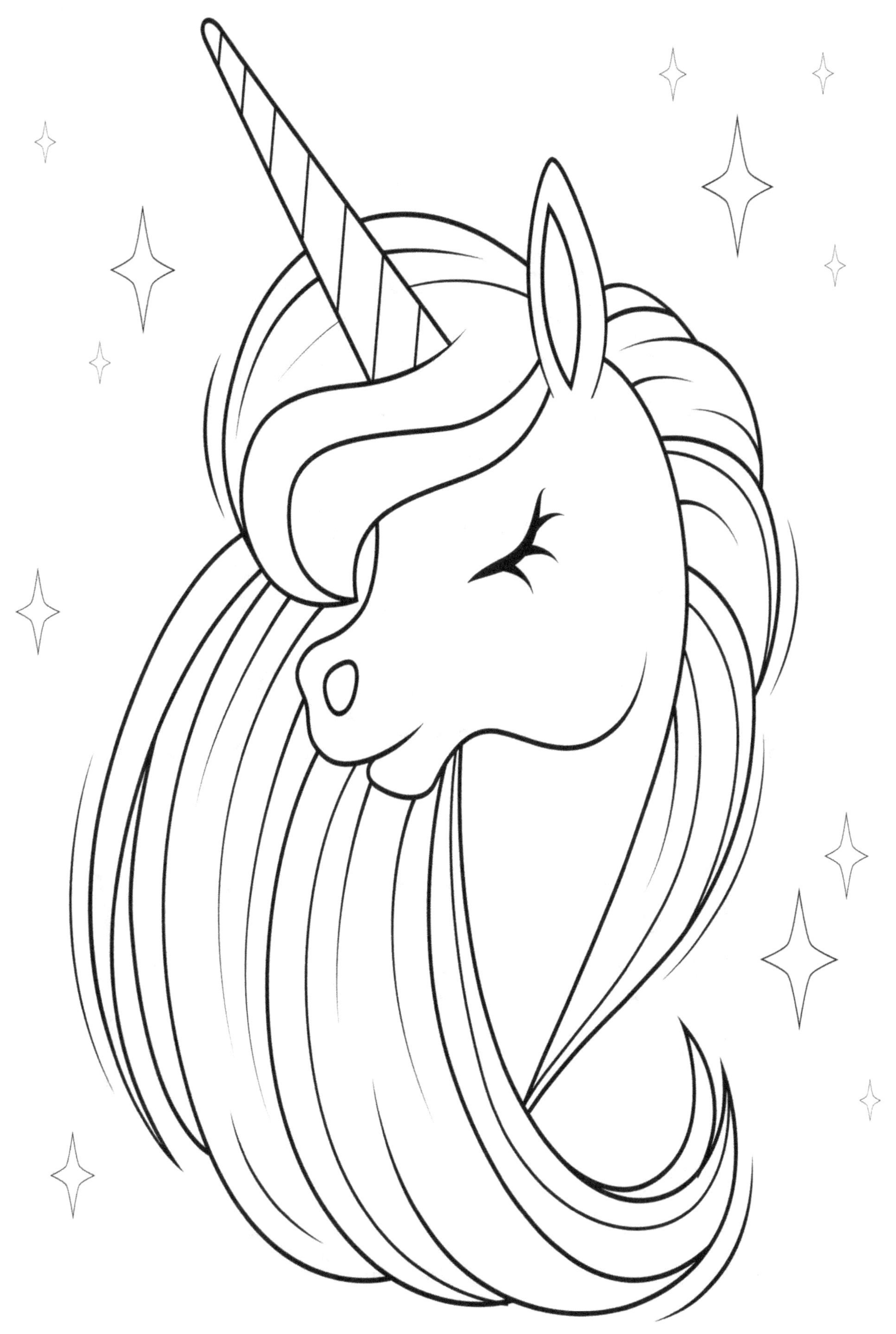

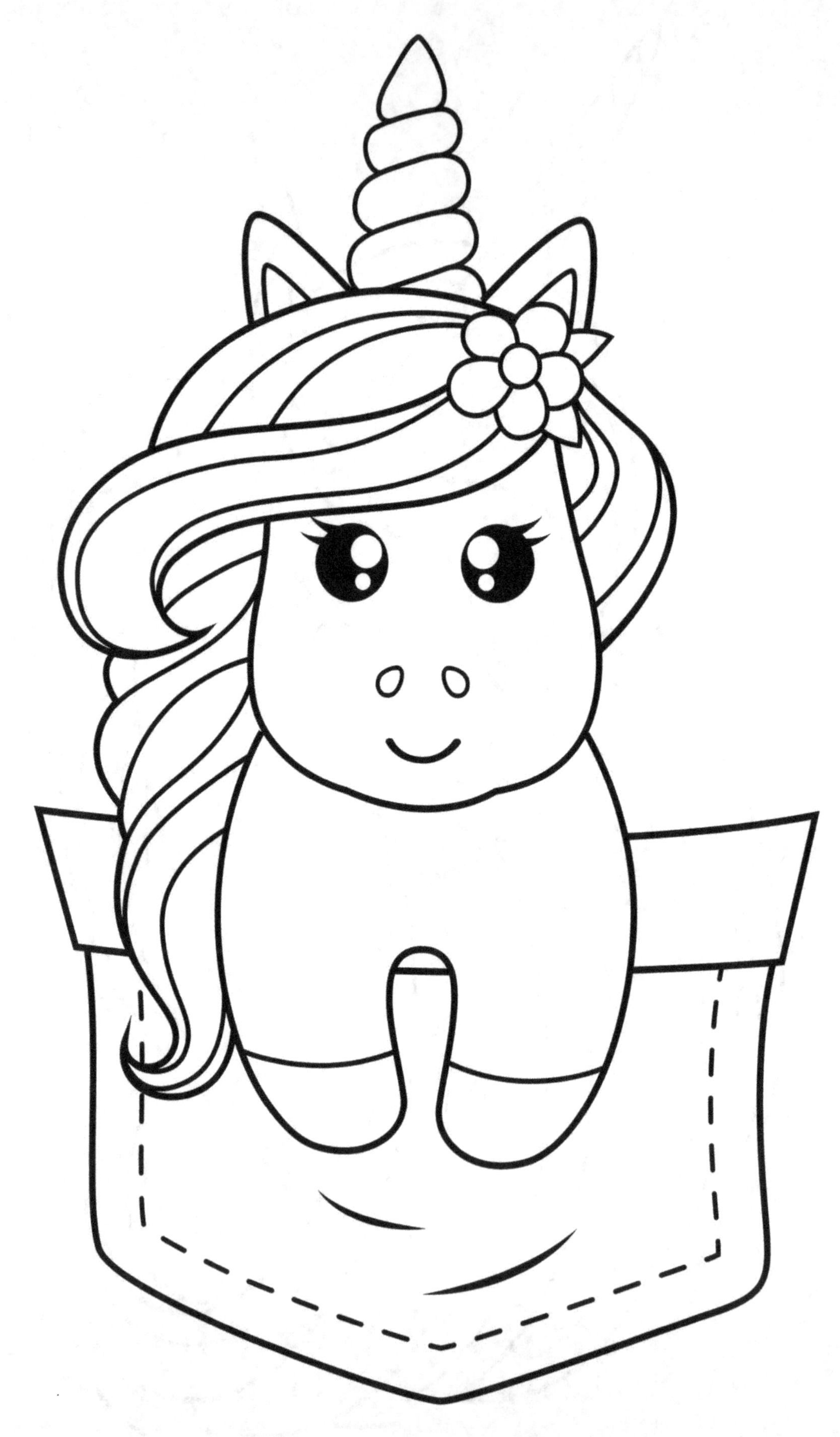

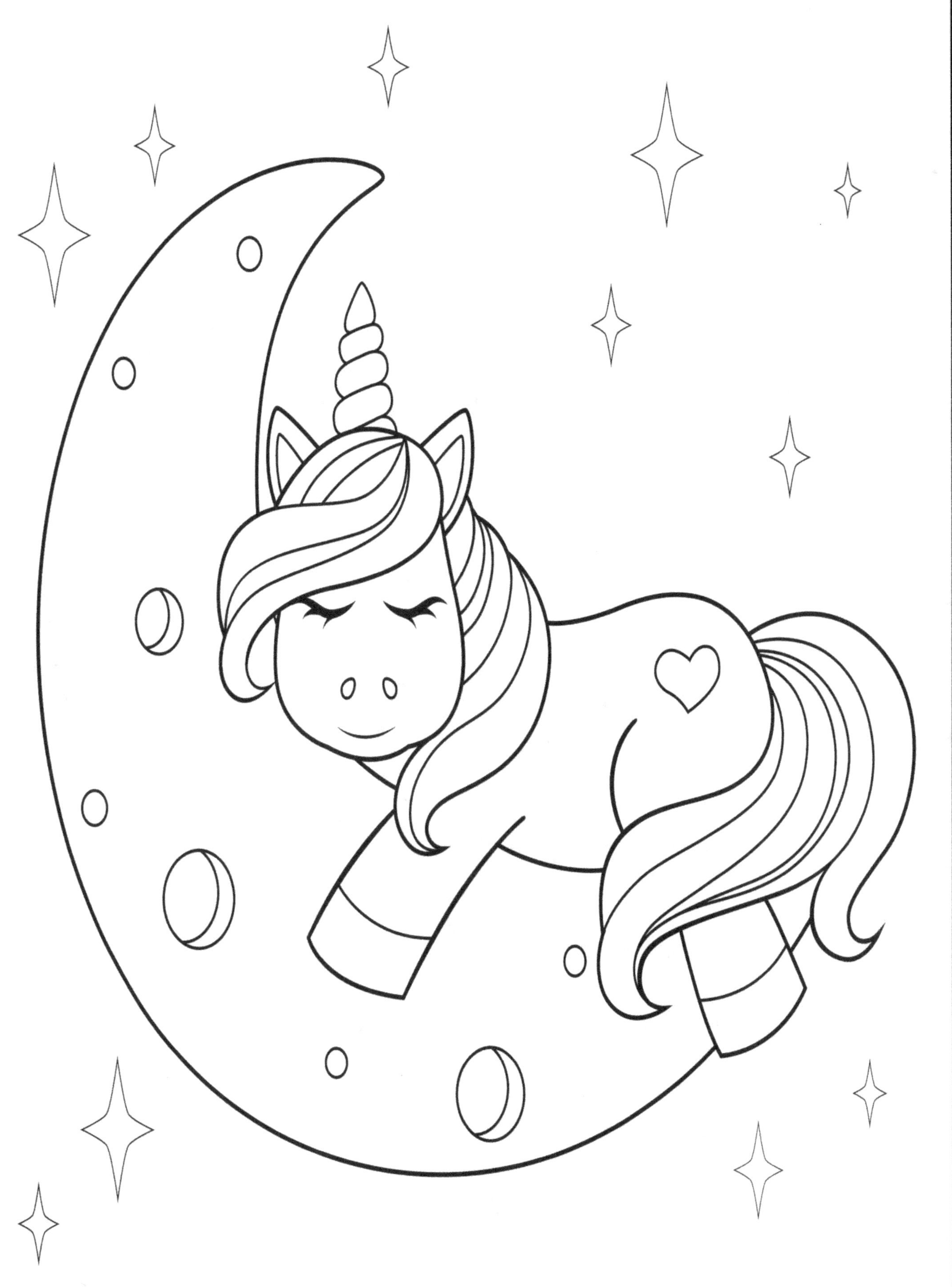

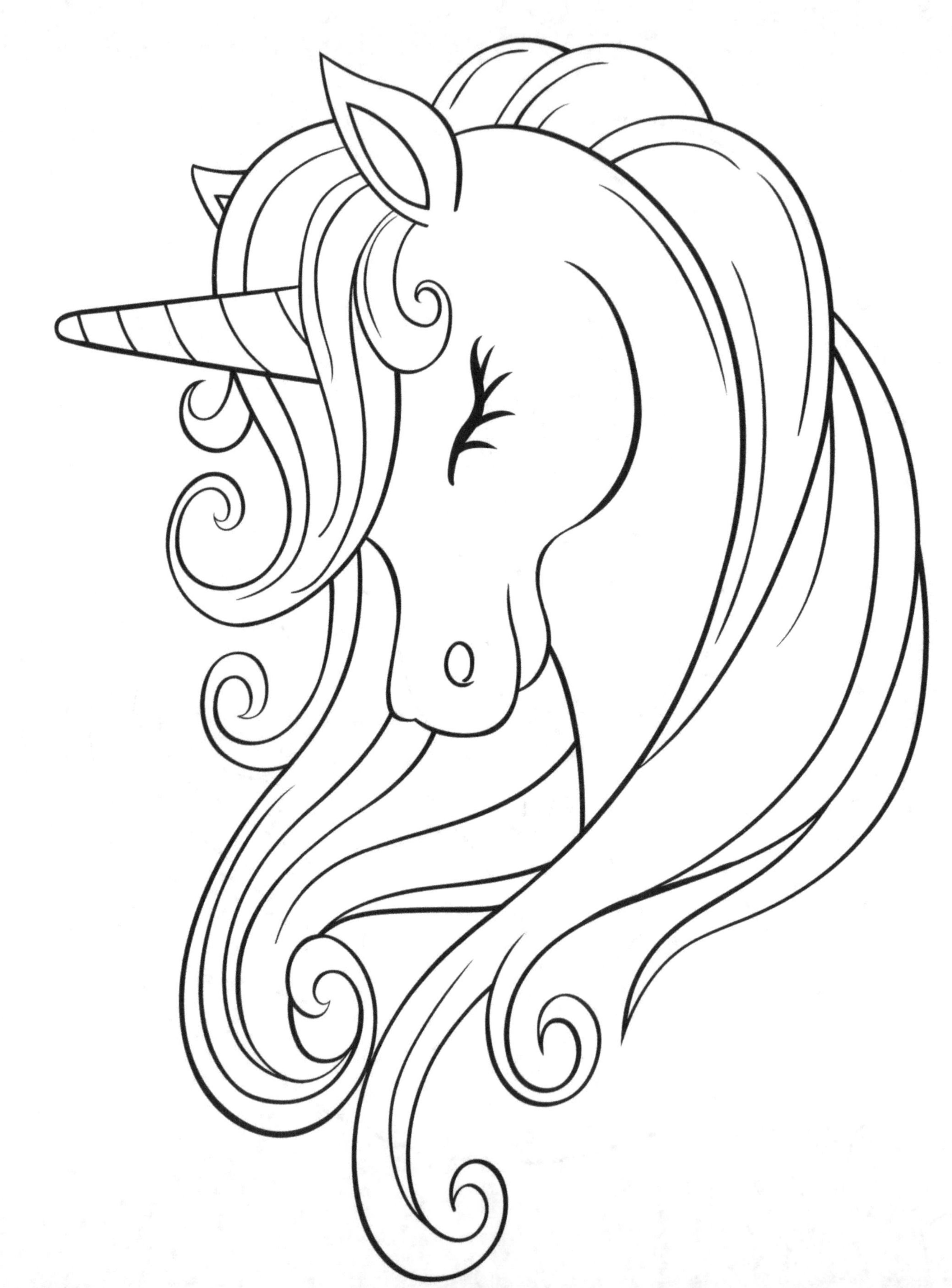

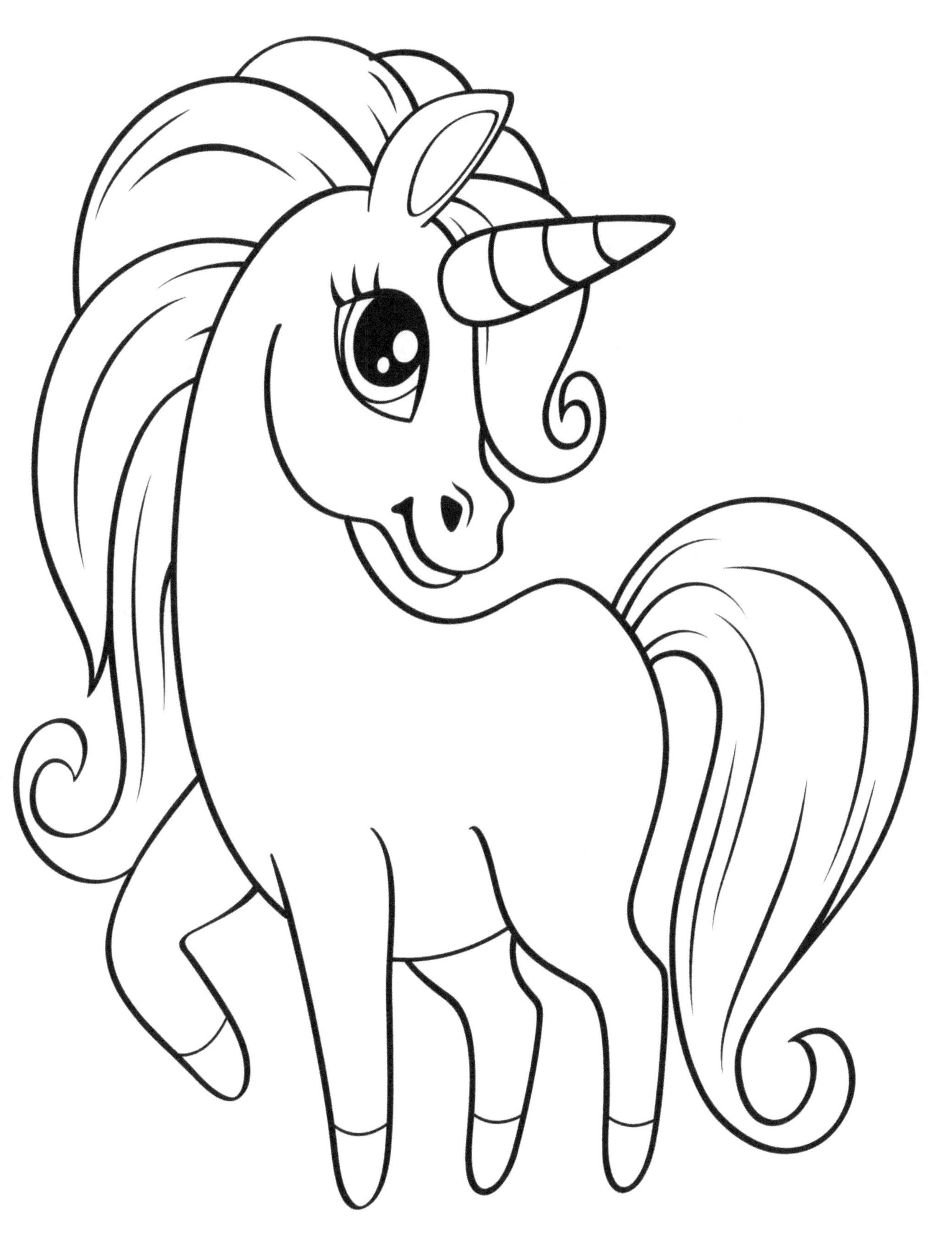

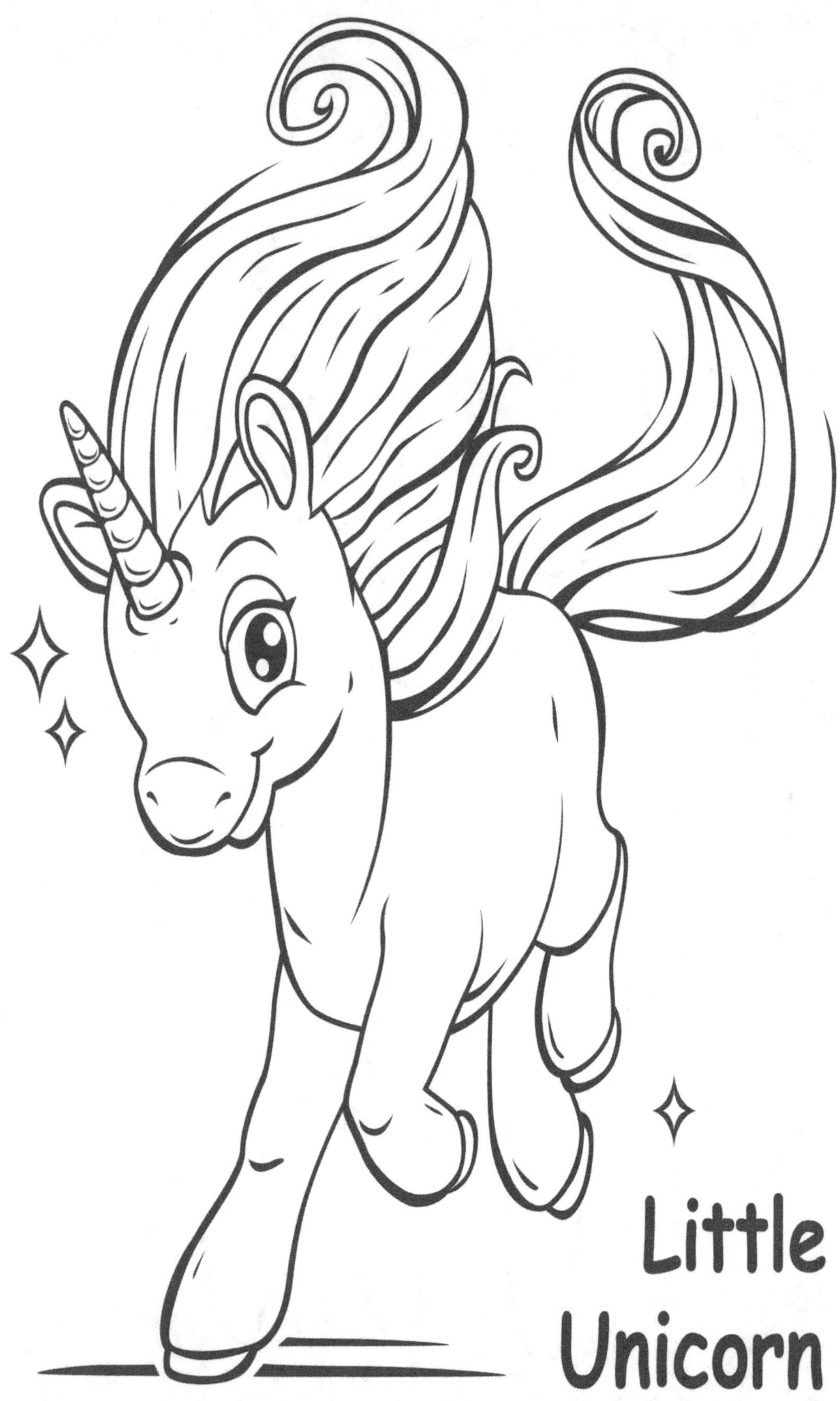

Little
Unicorn

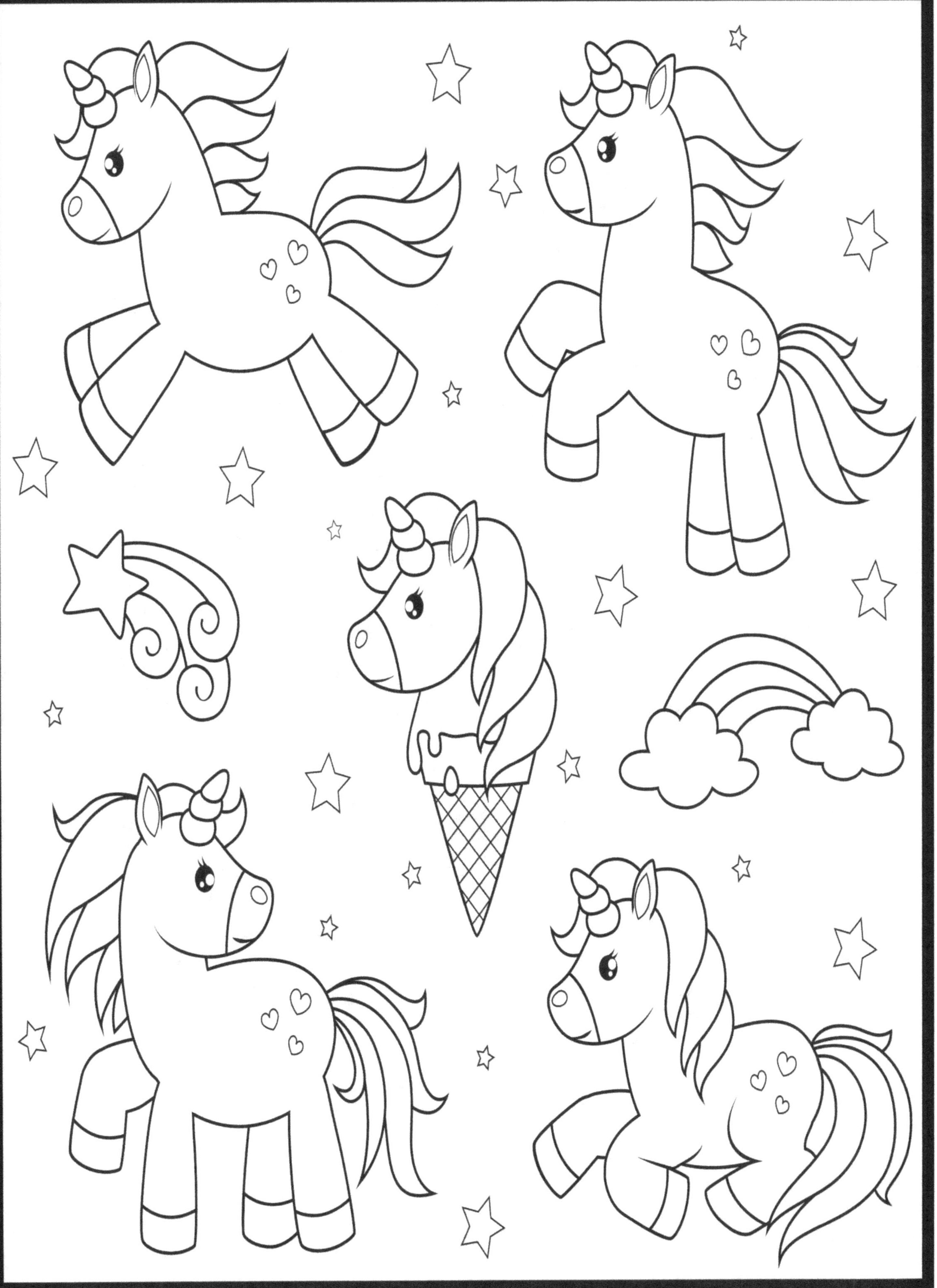

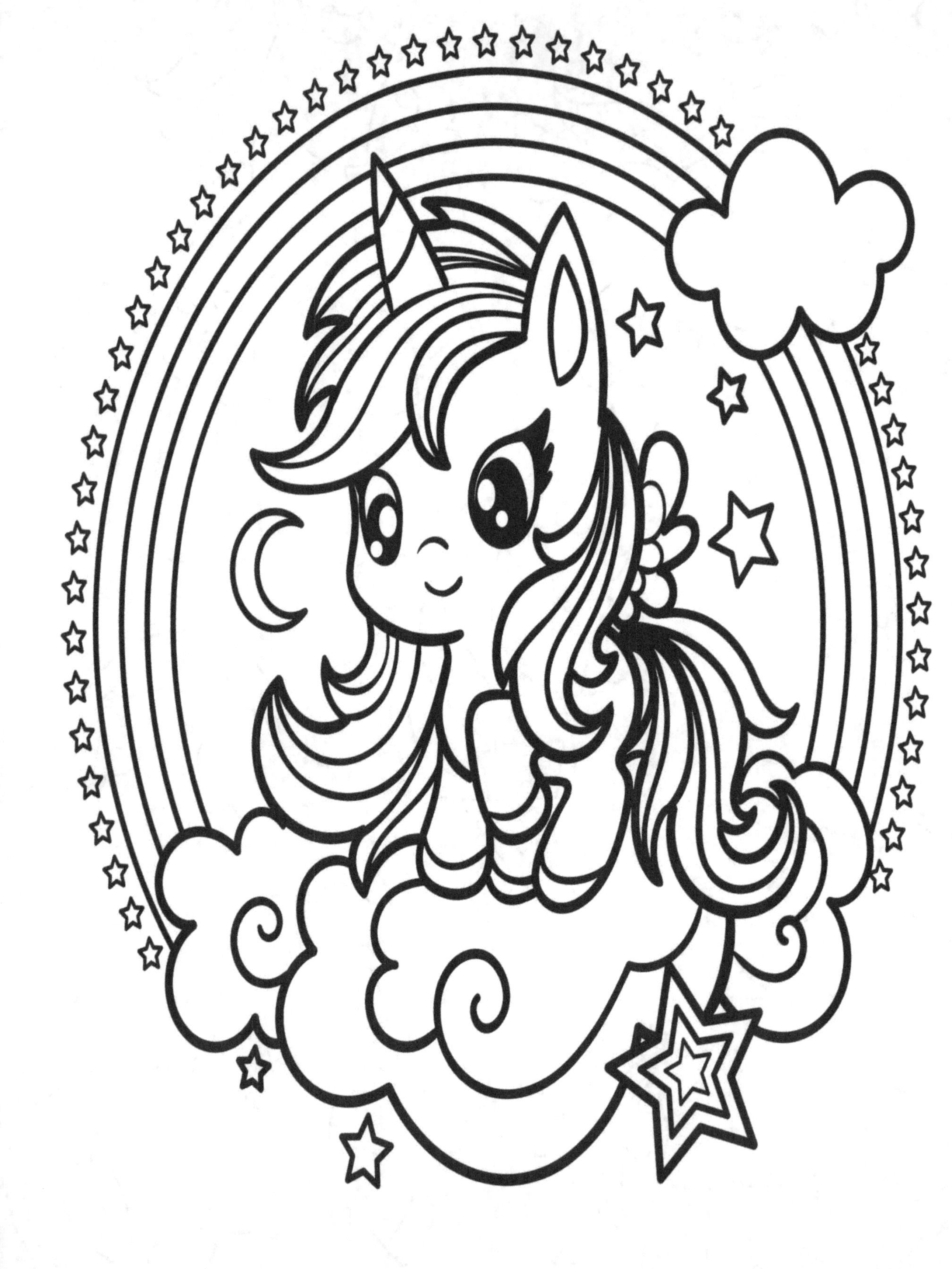

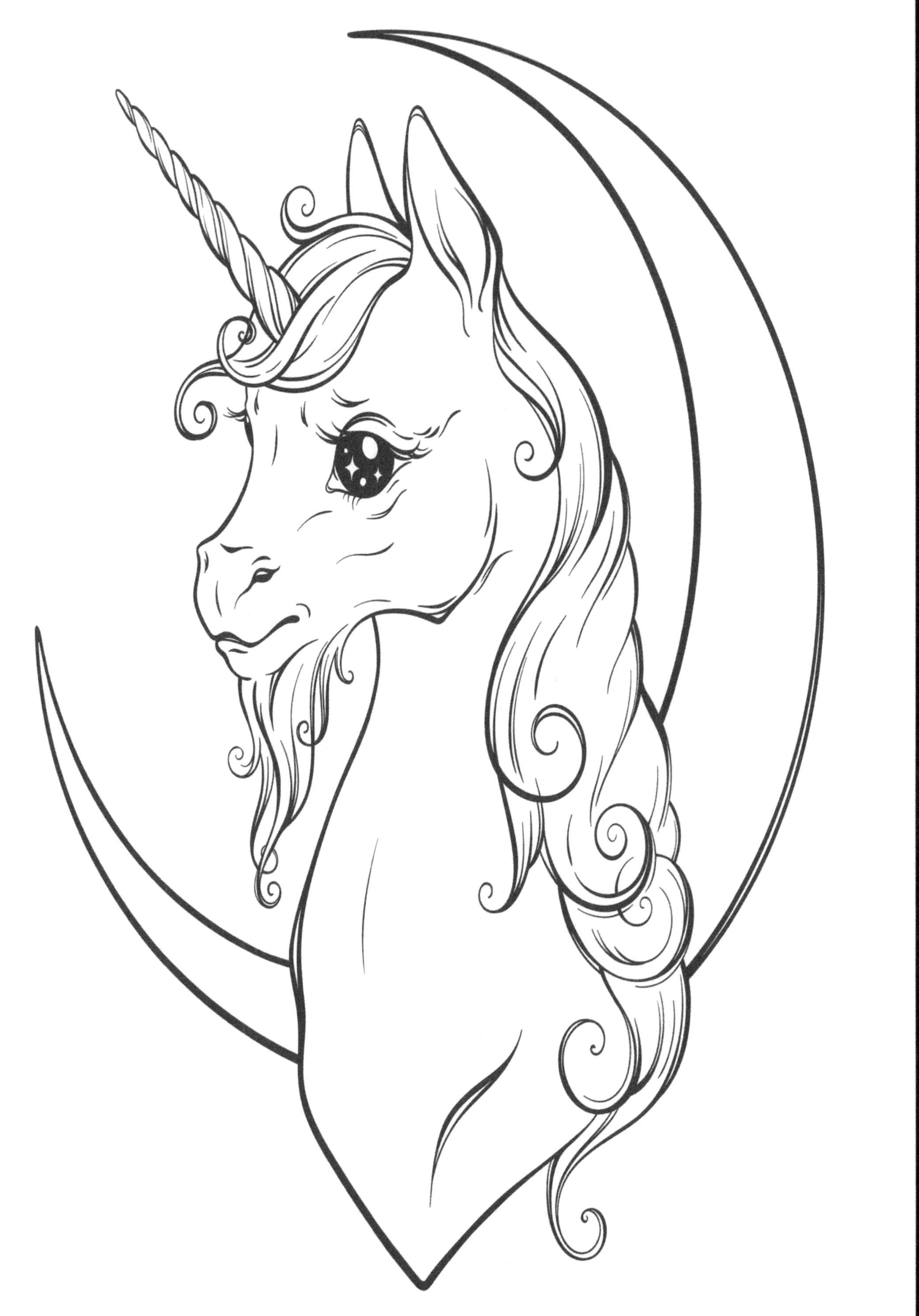

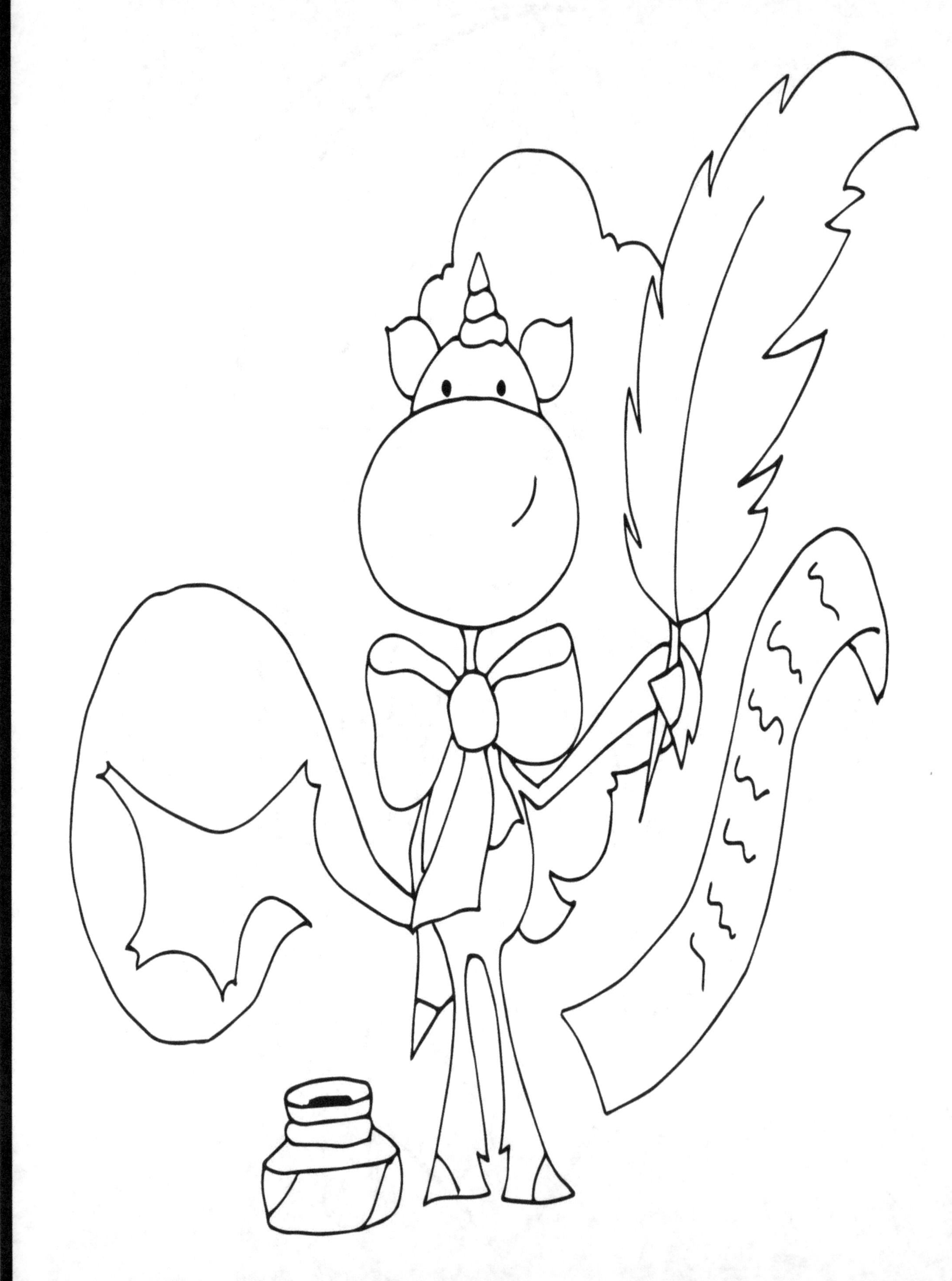

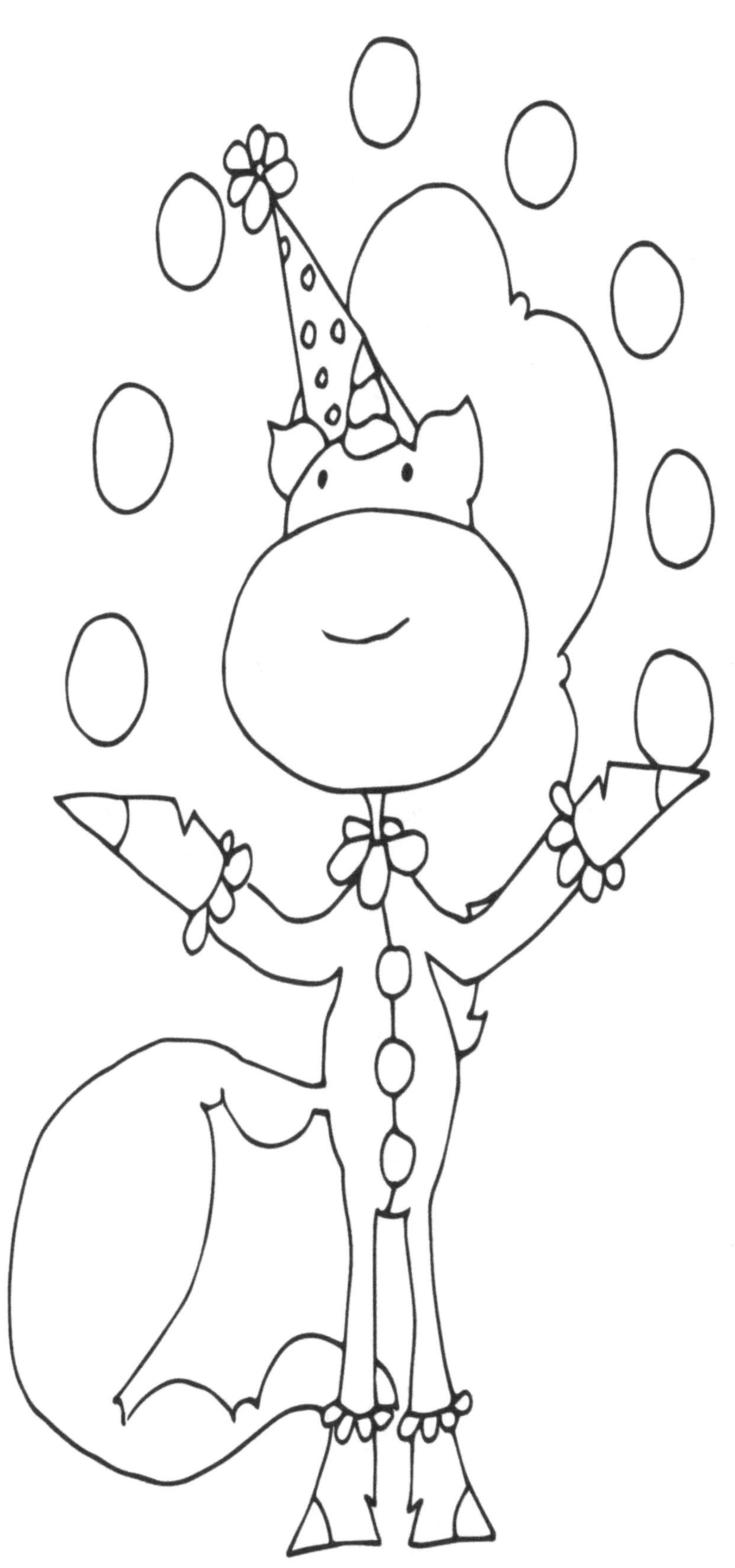

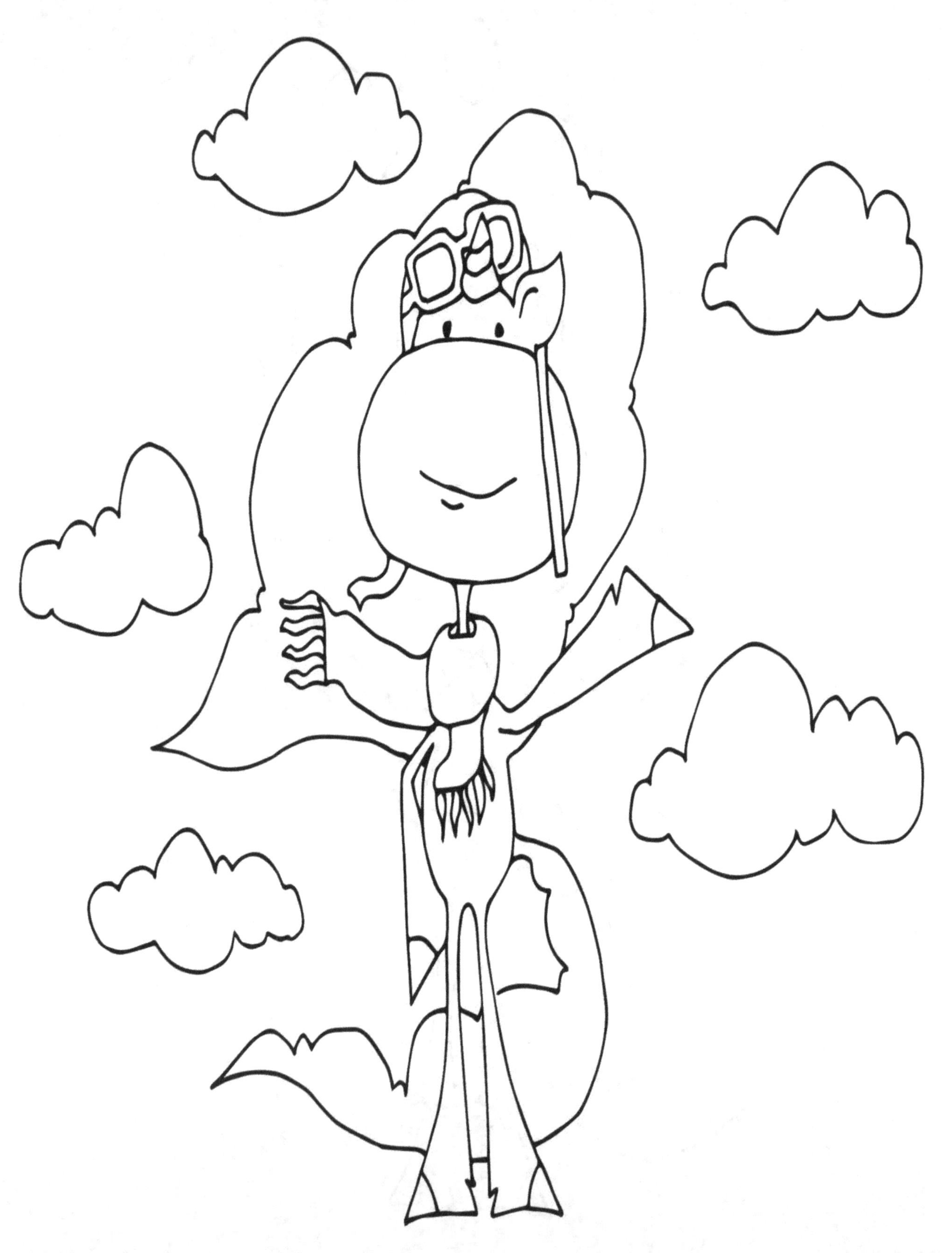

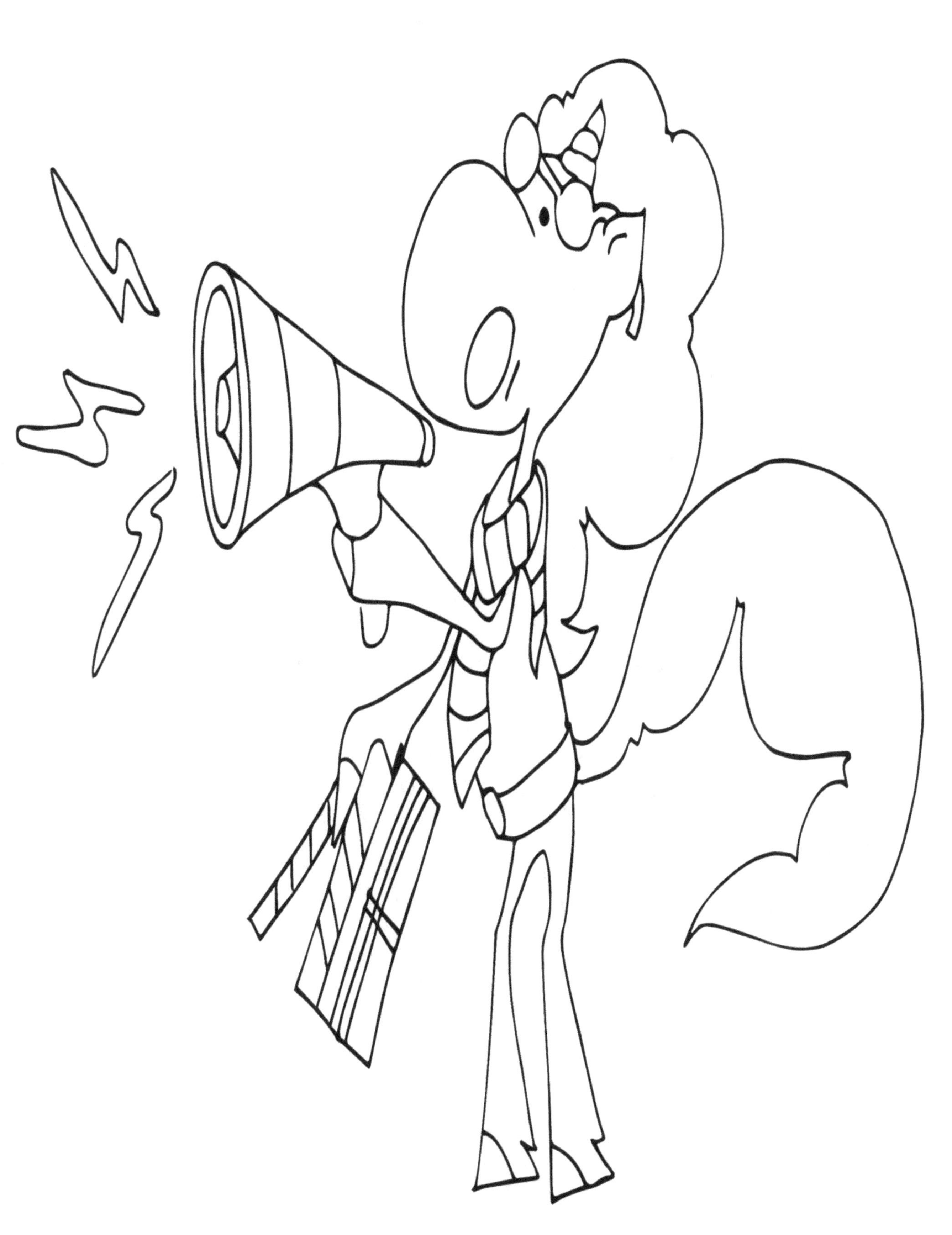

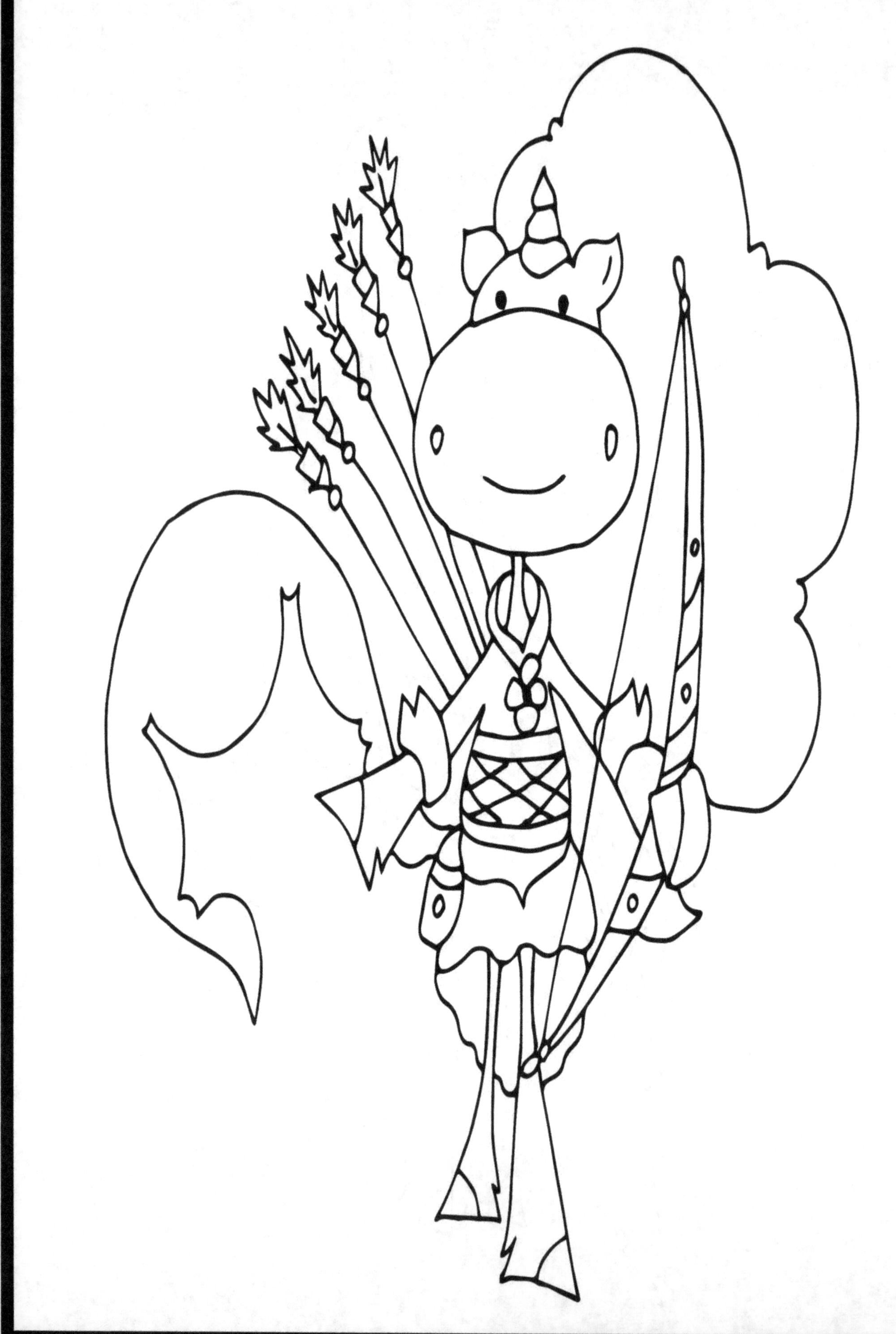

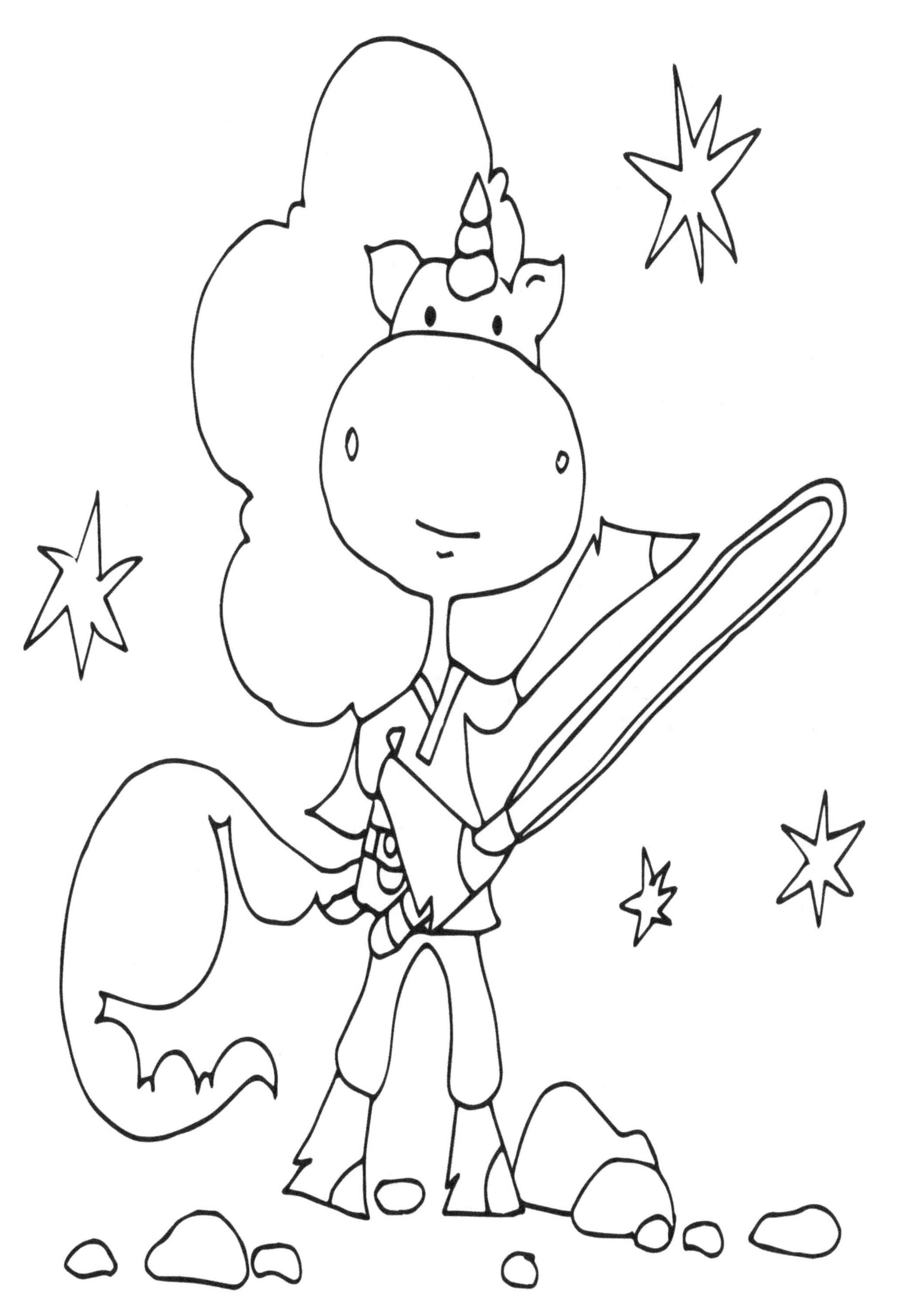

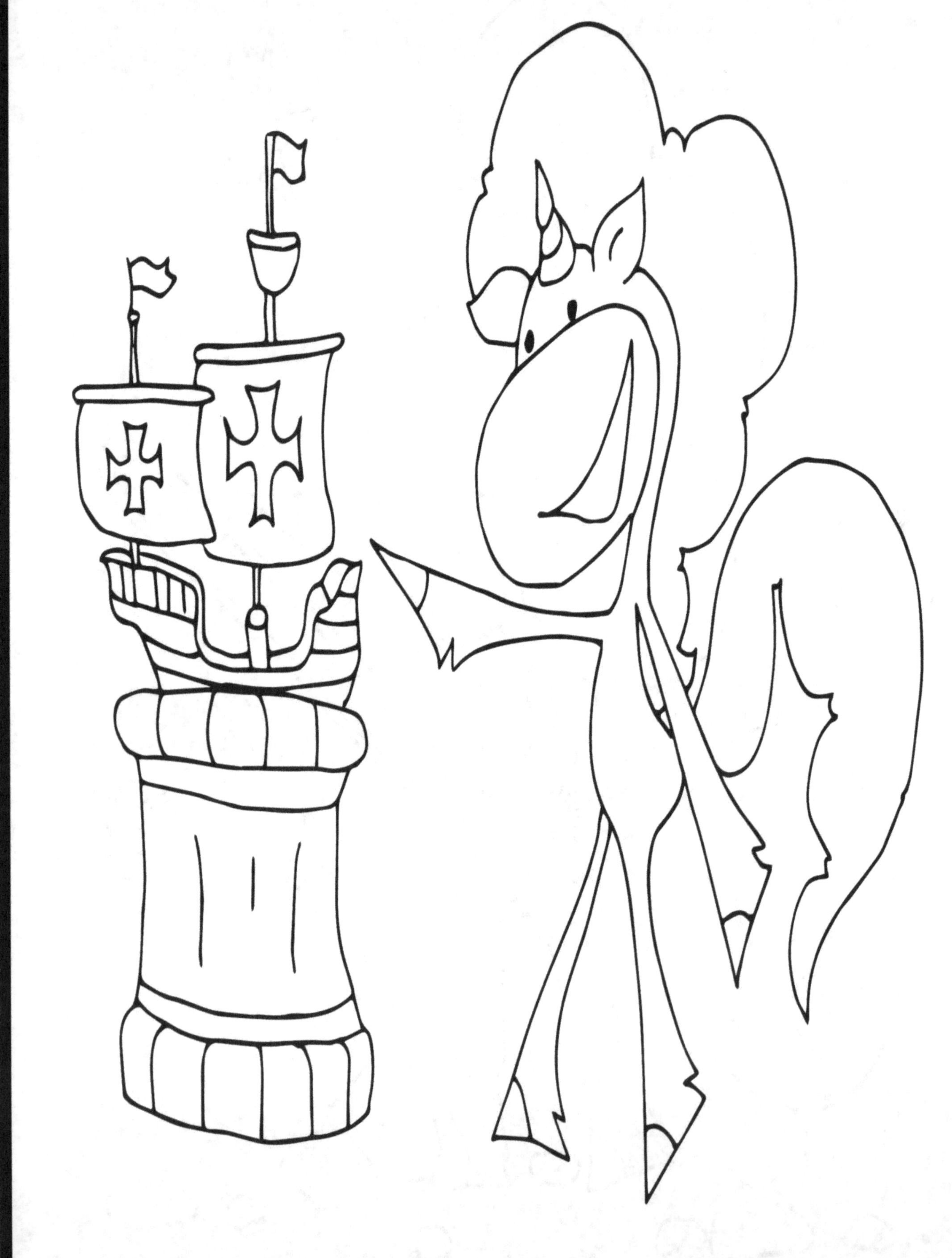

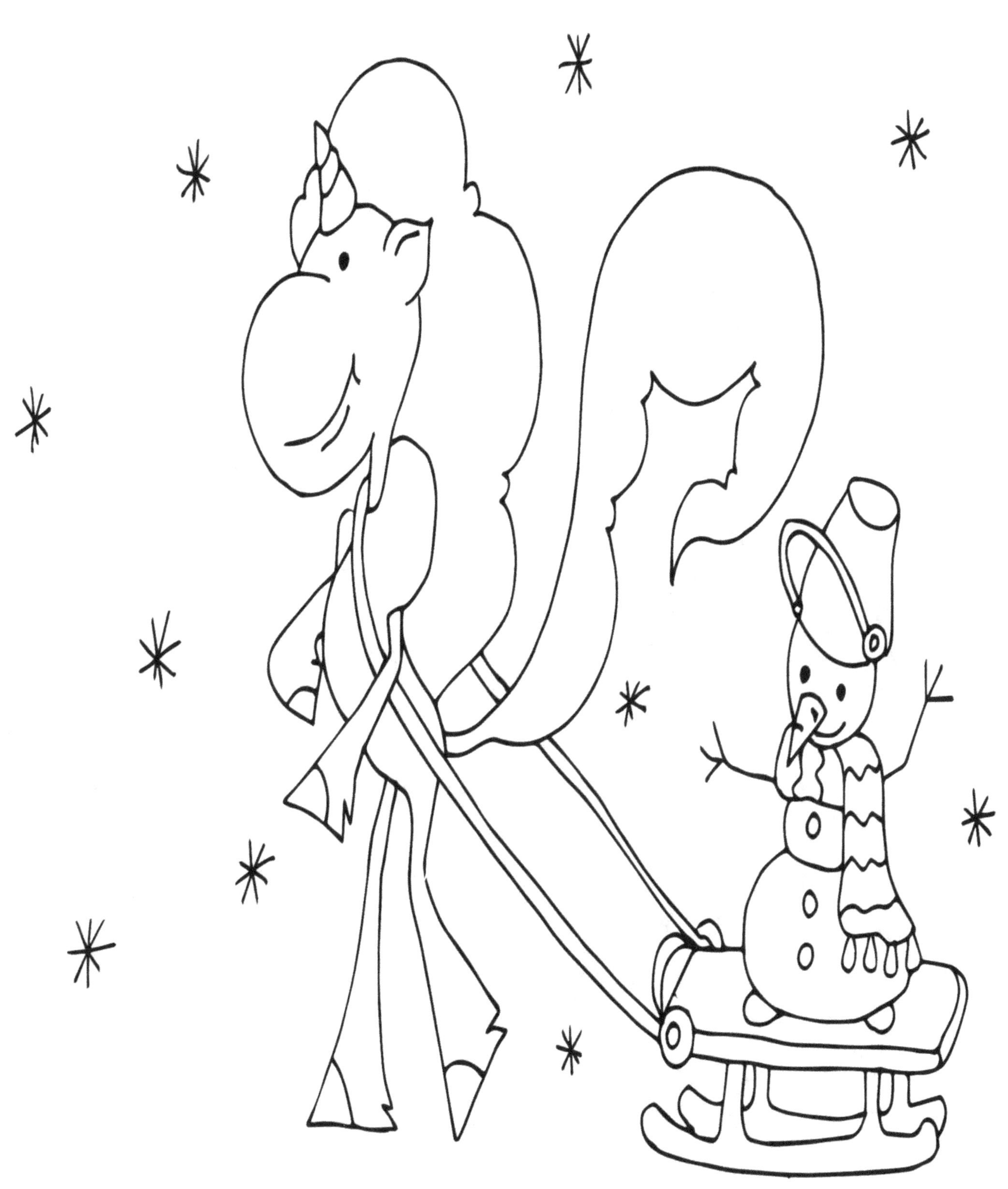

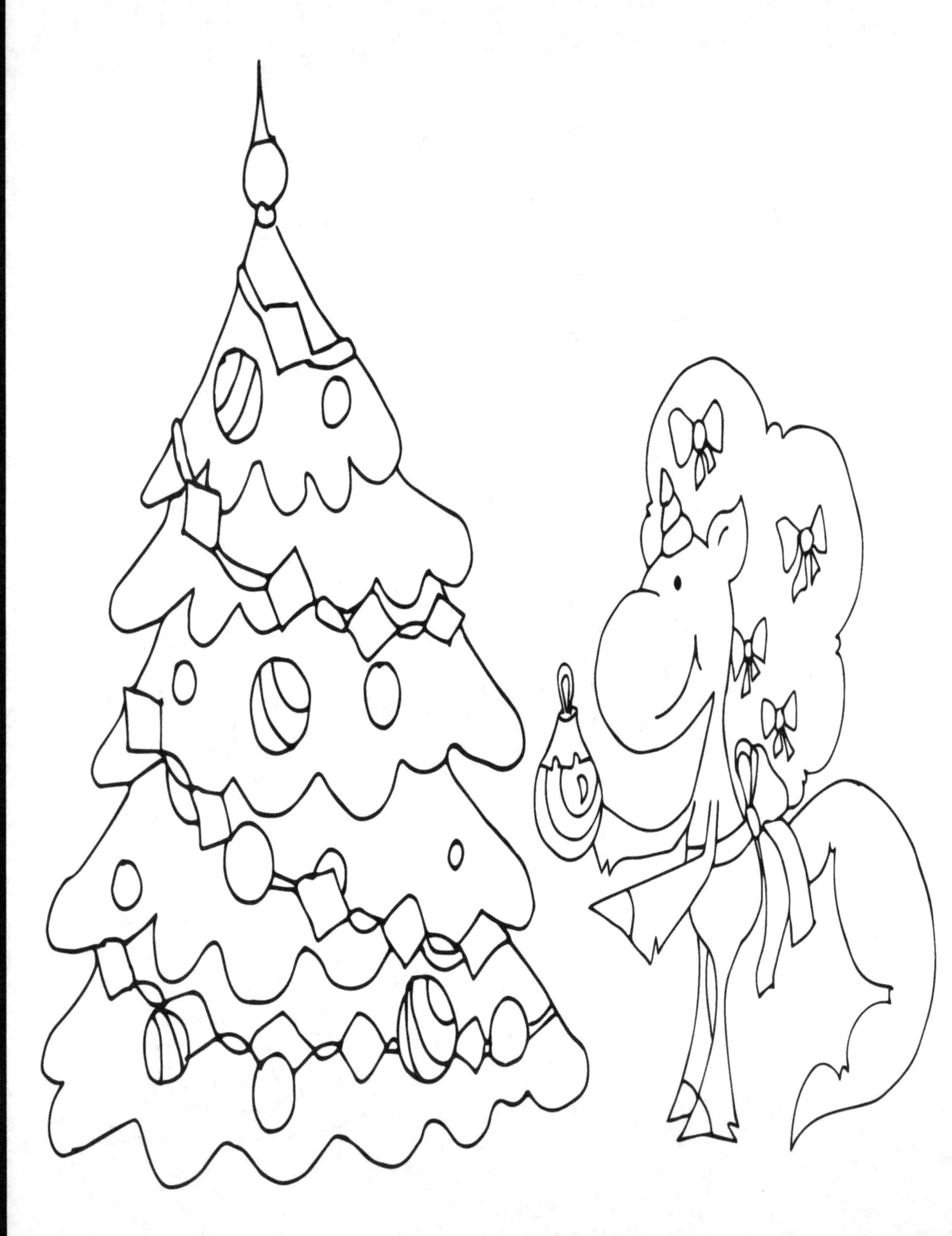

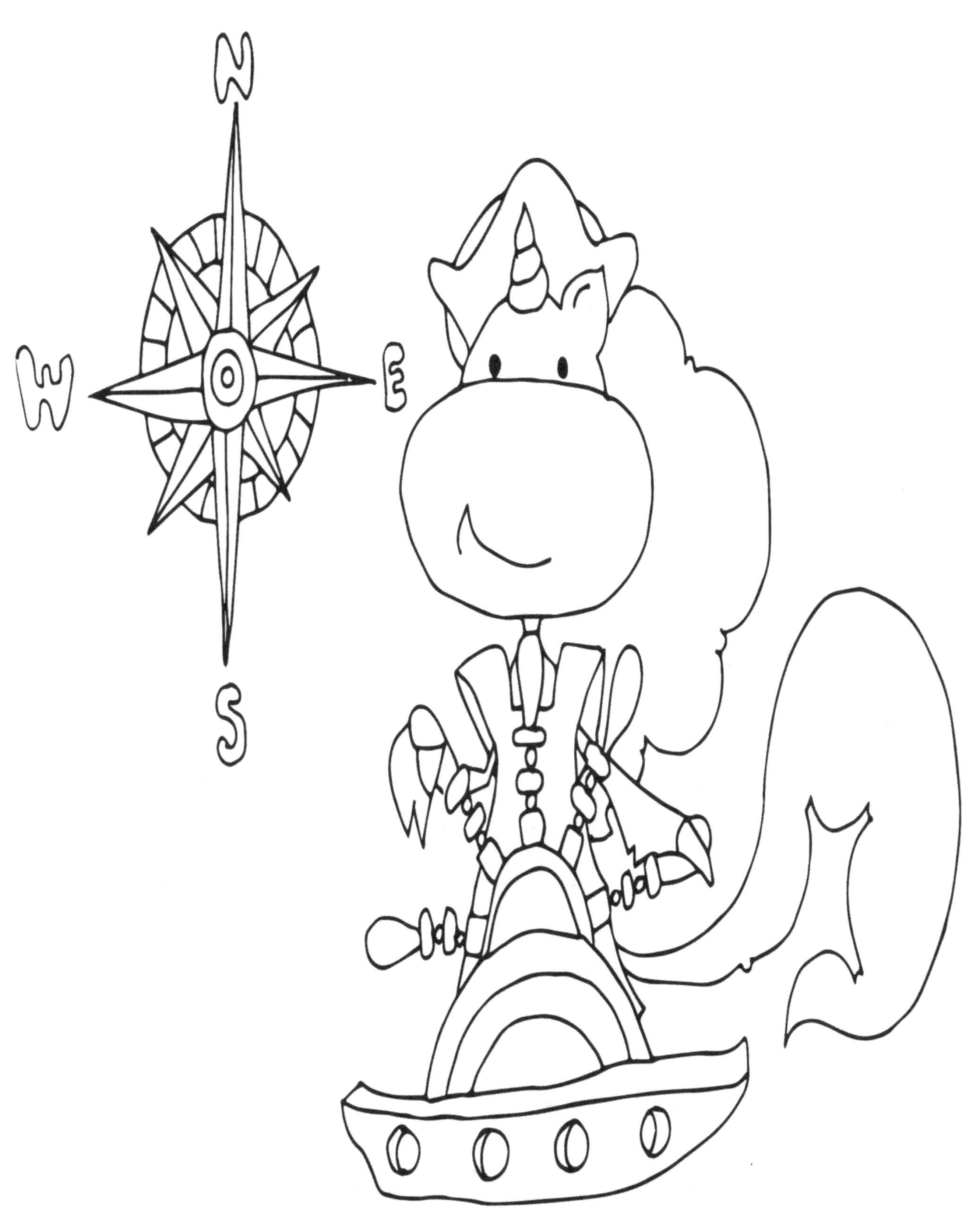
N
W
E
S

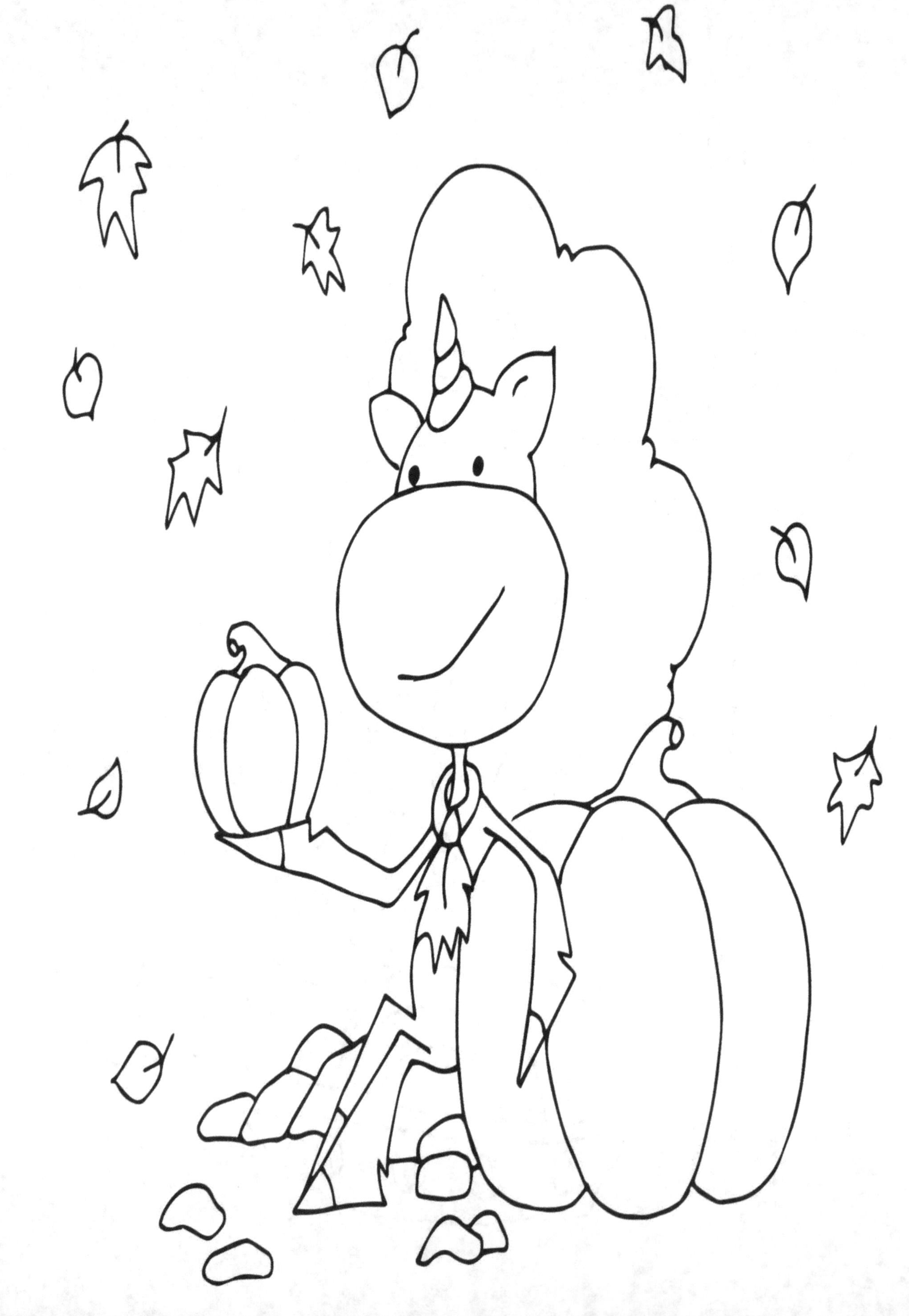

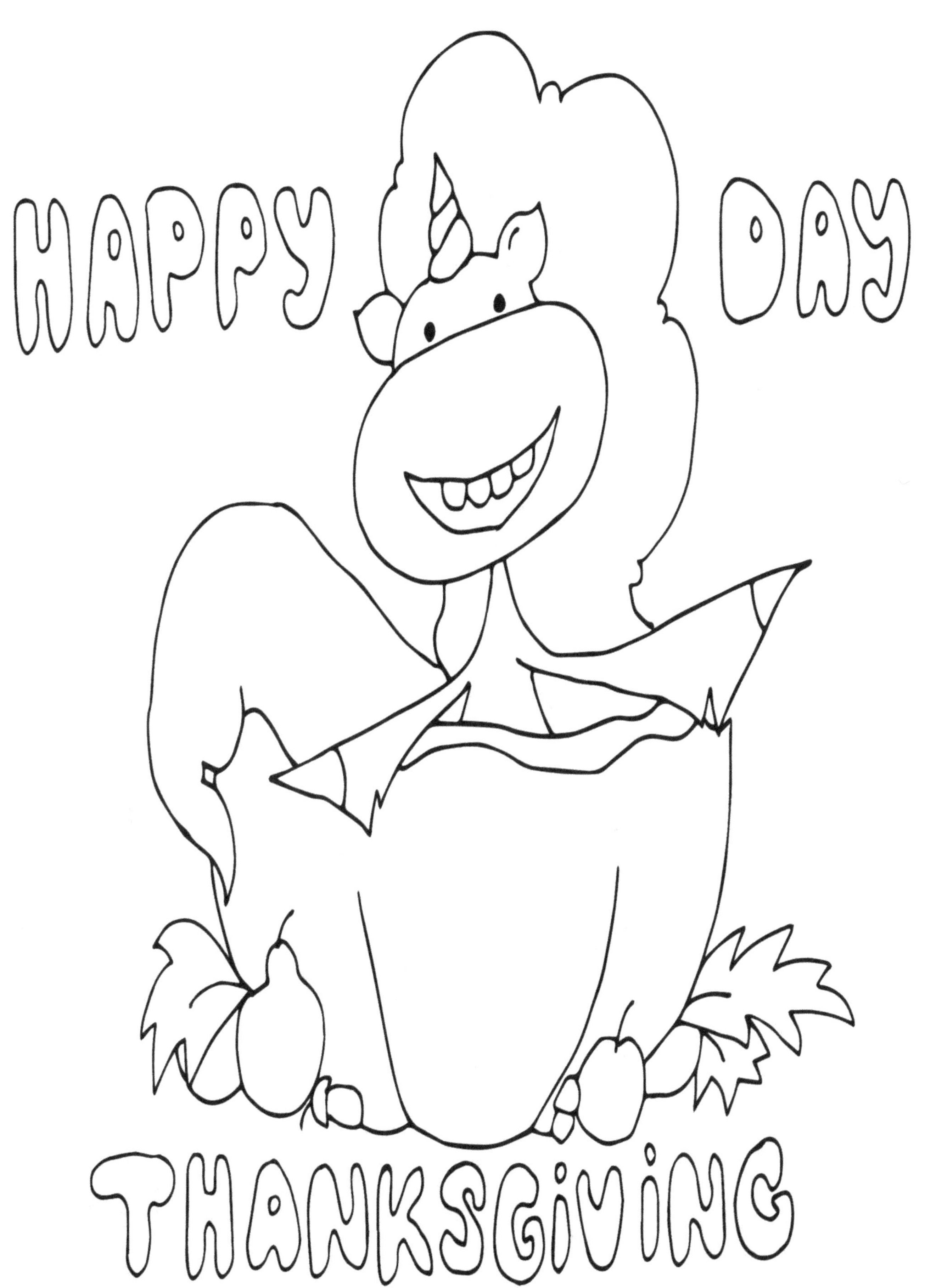

HAPPY DAY
THANKSGIVING

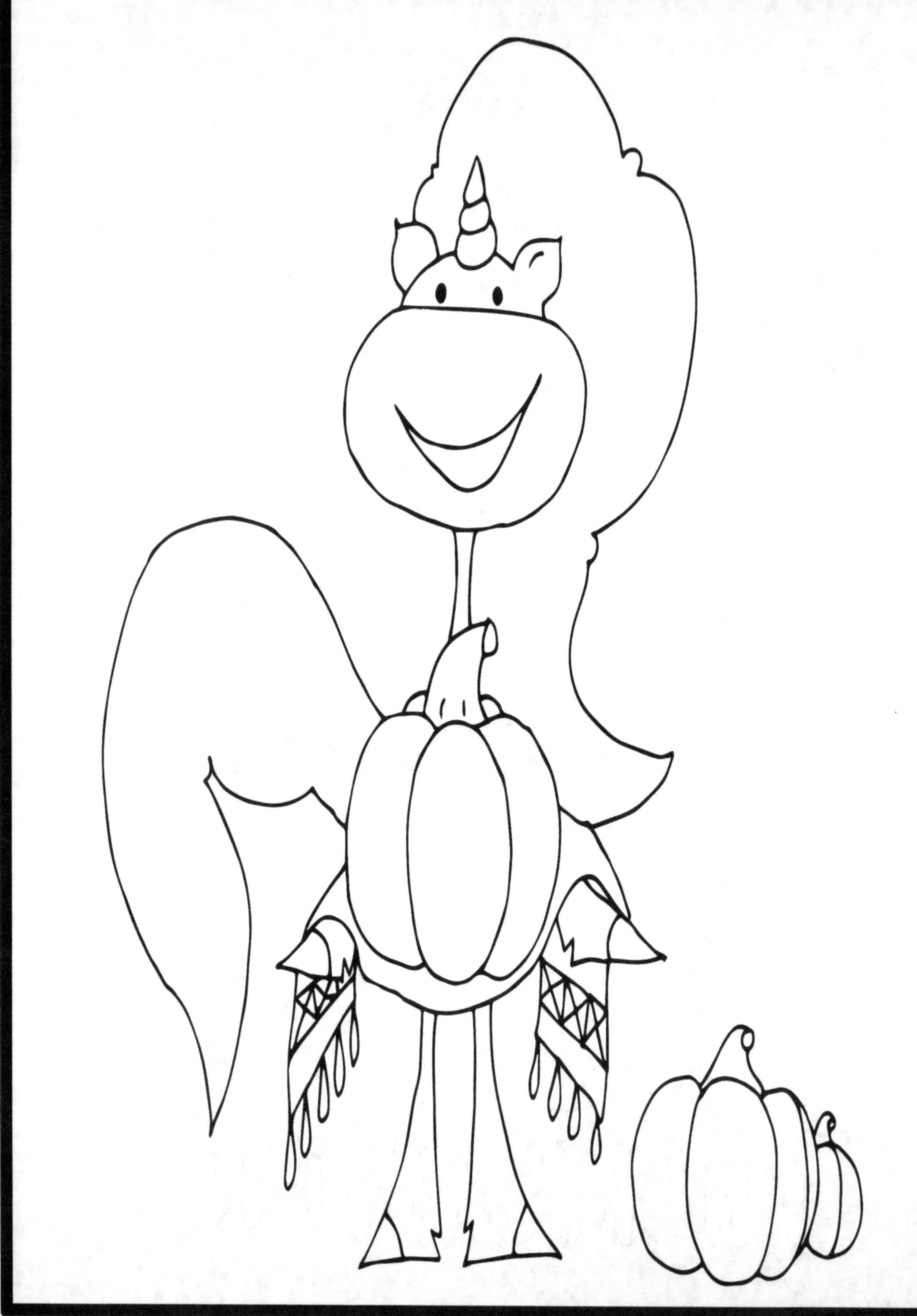

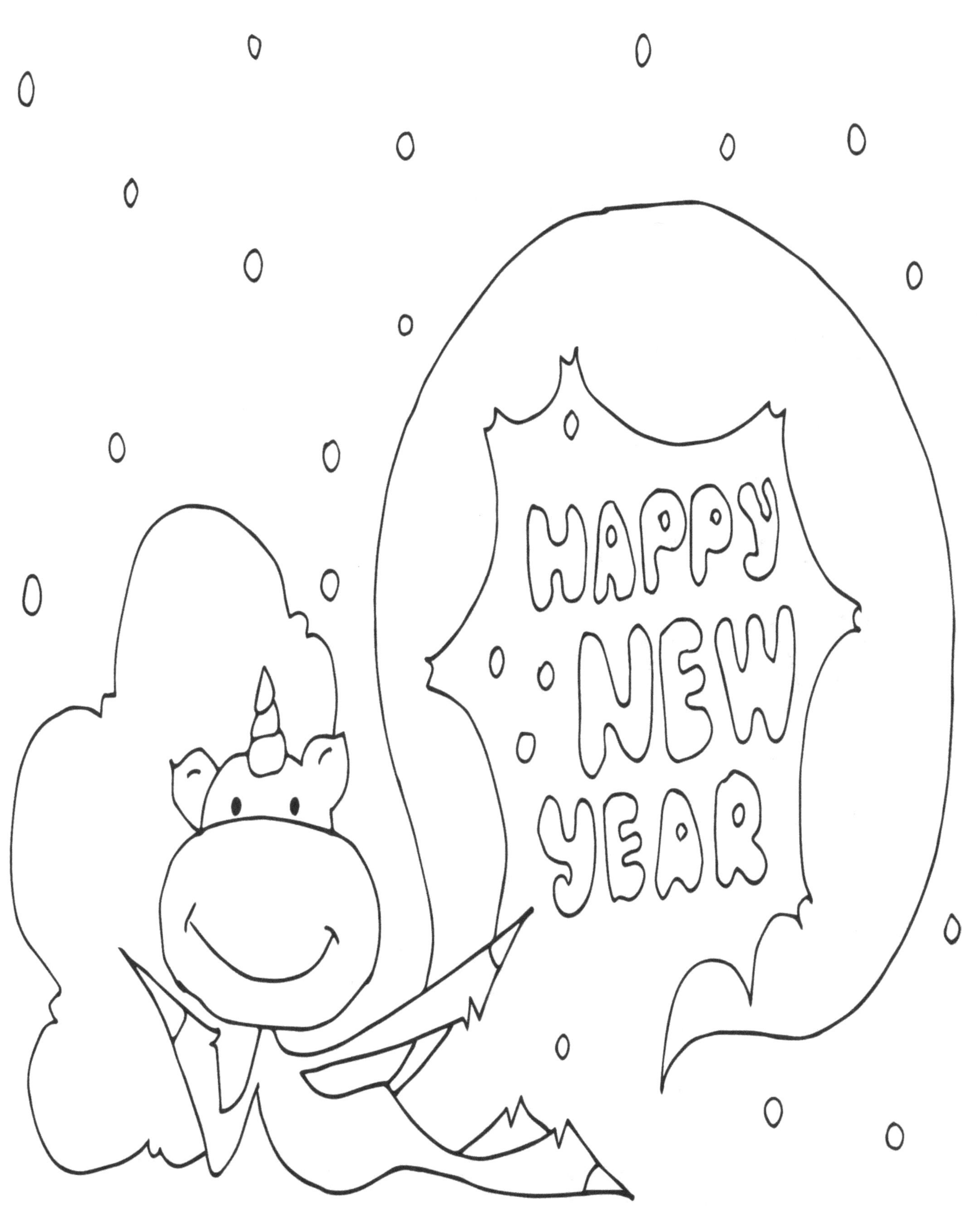

HAPPY
NEW
YEAR

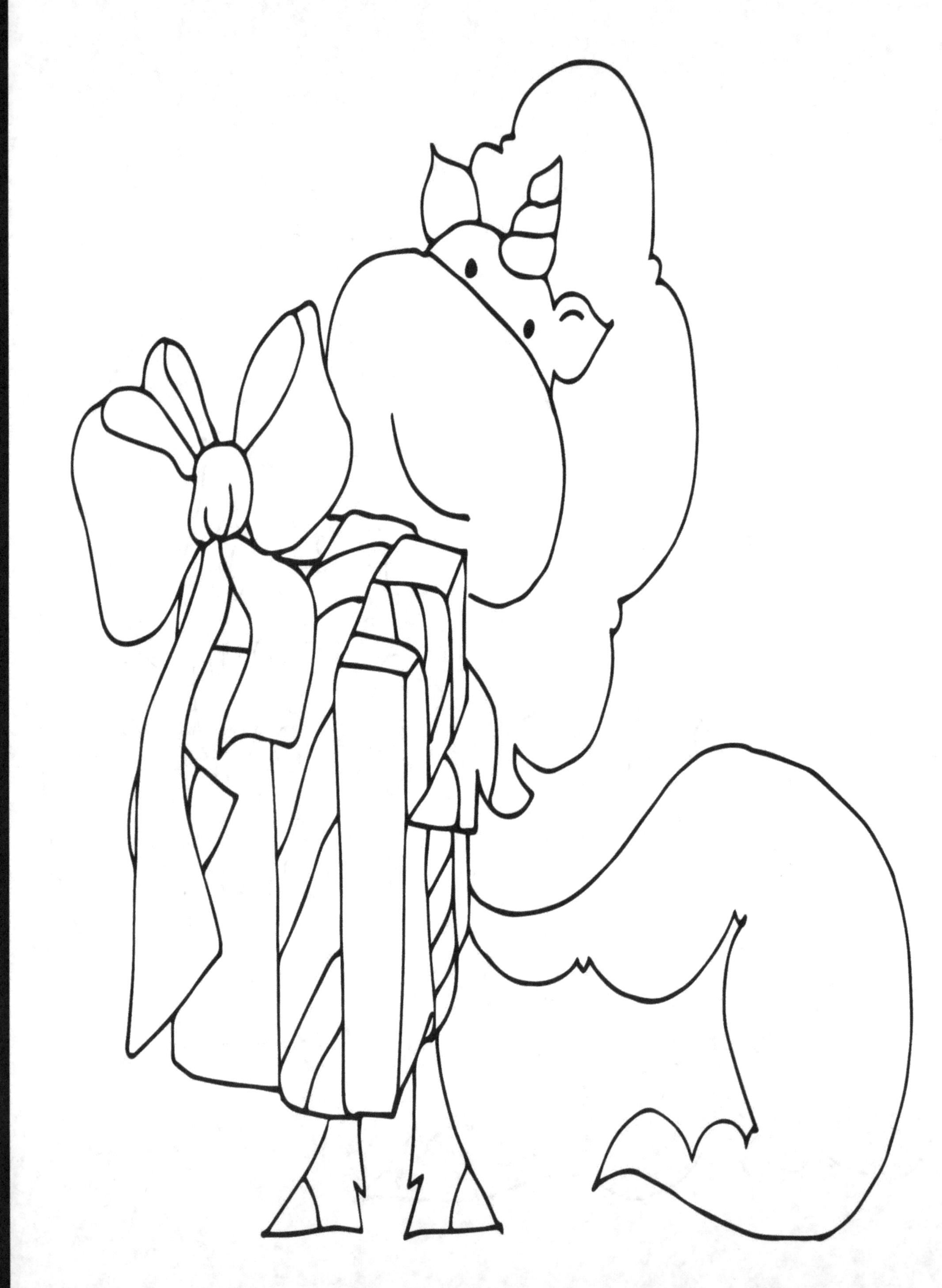

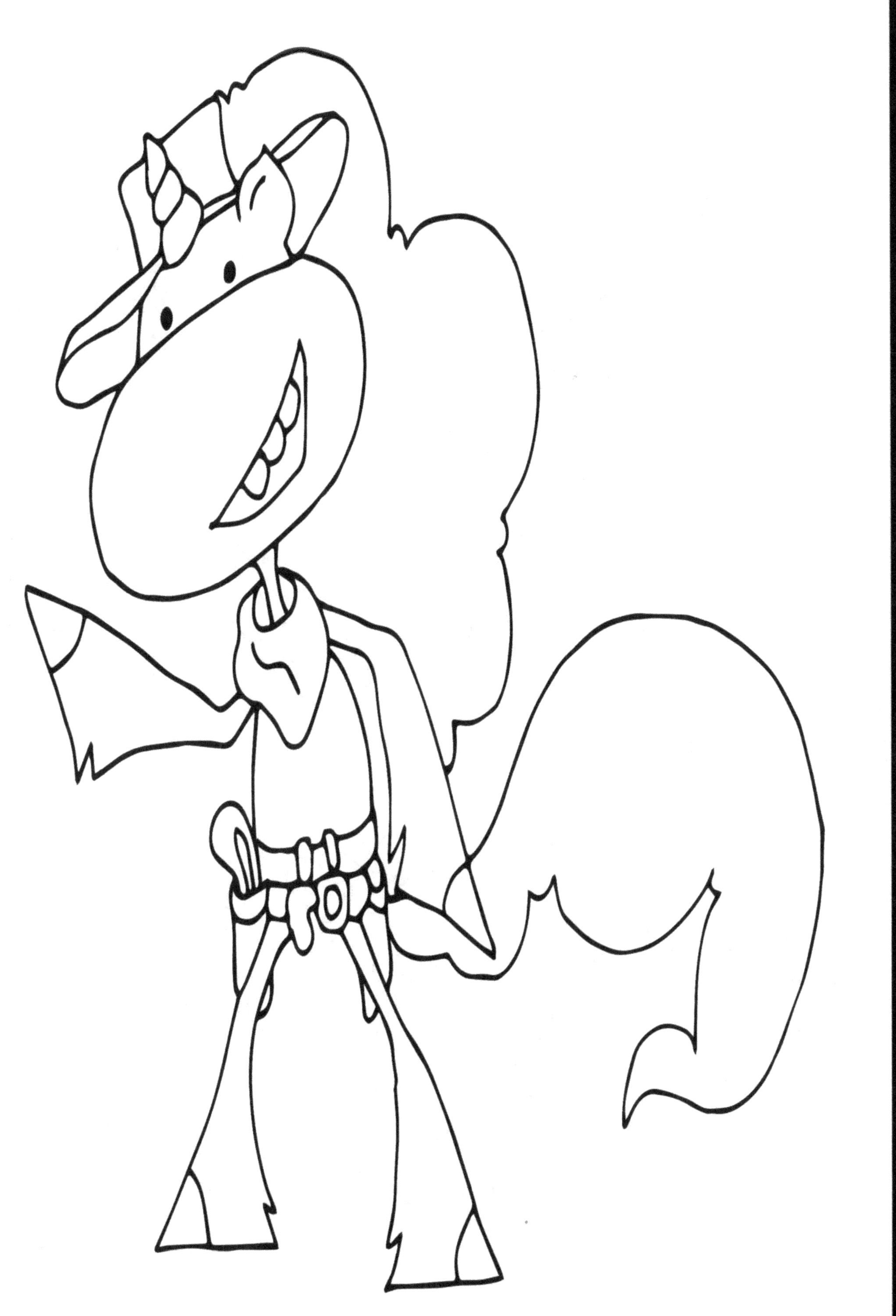

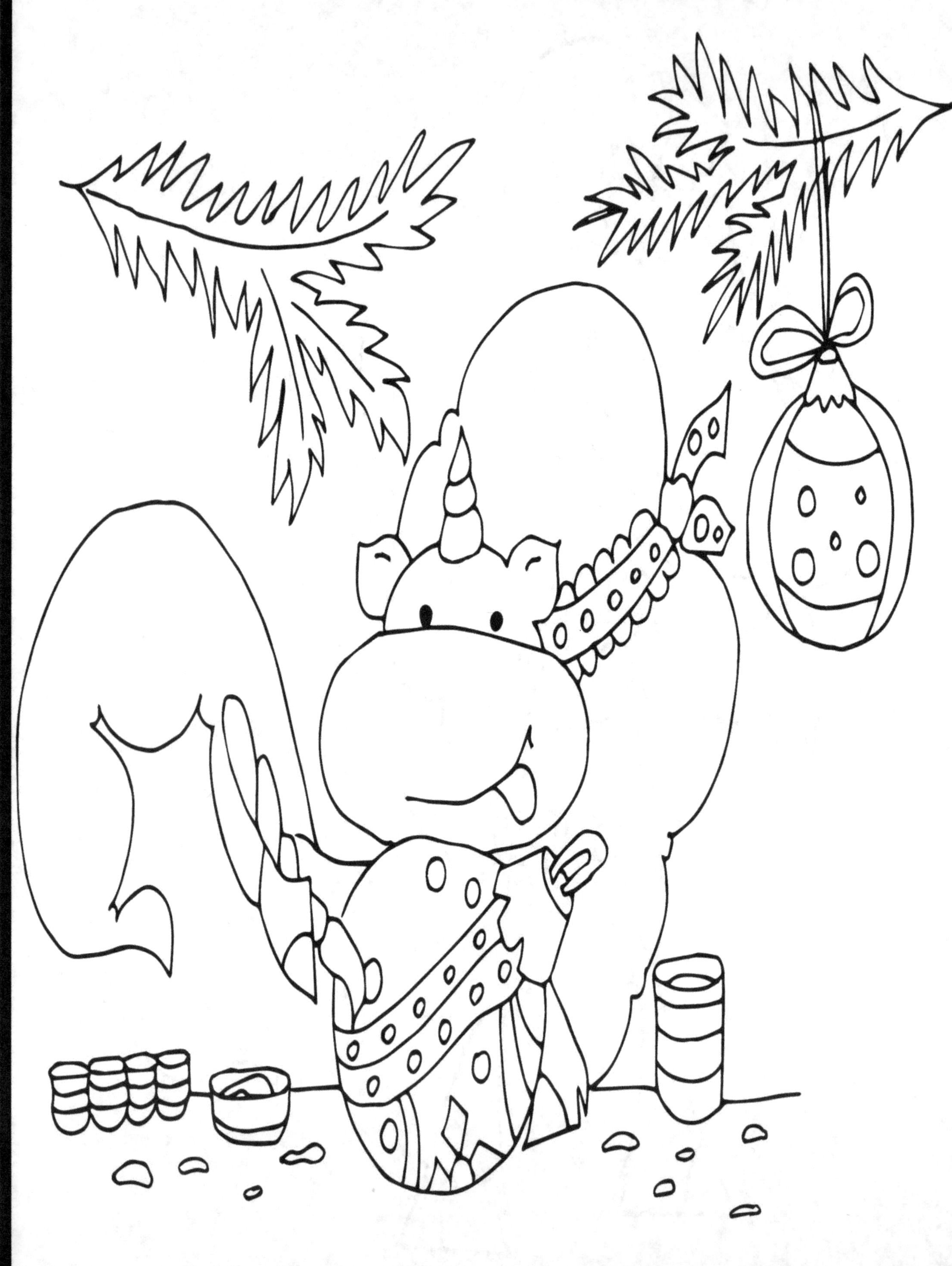

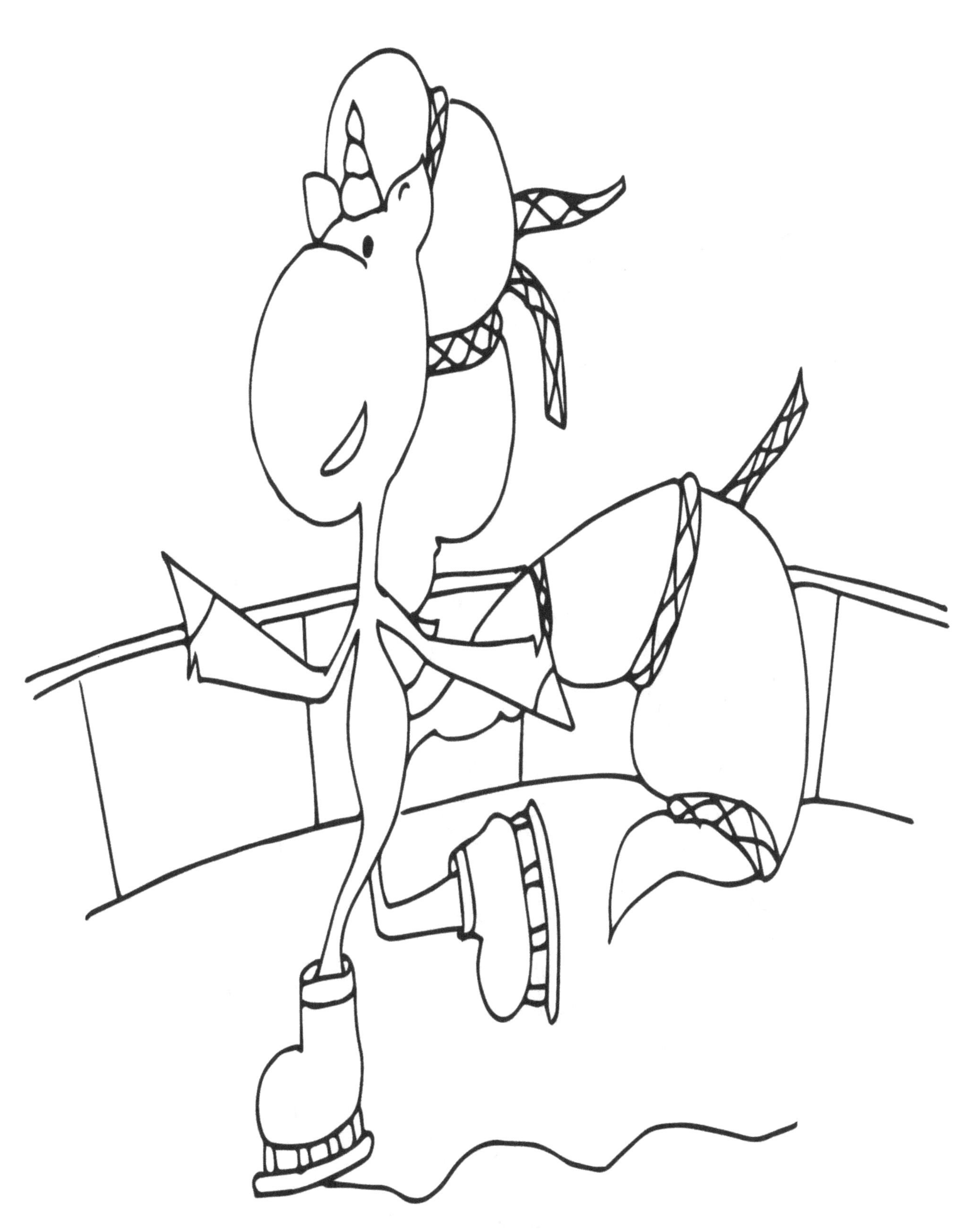

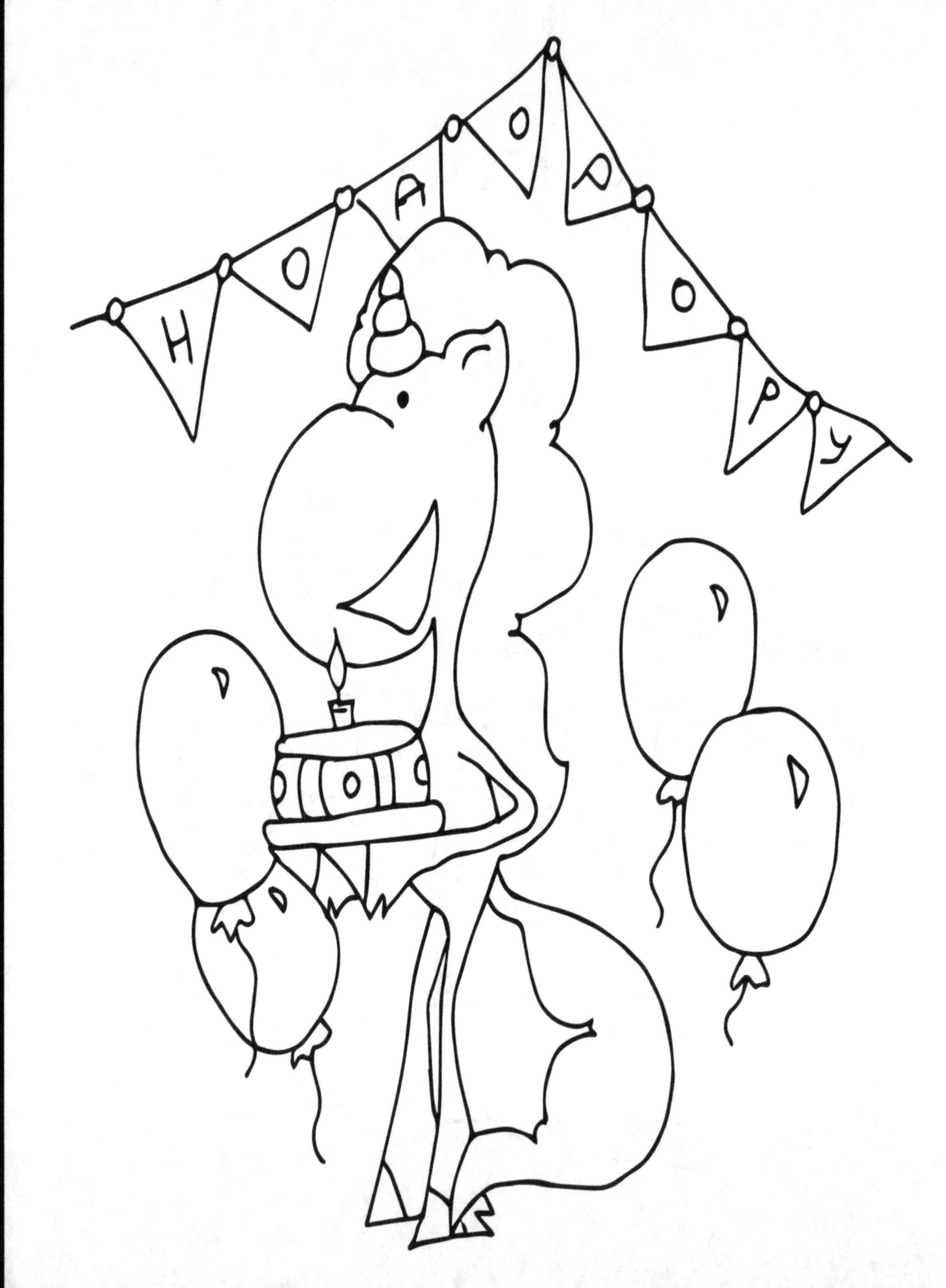

H
A
P
P
Y

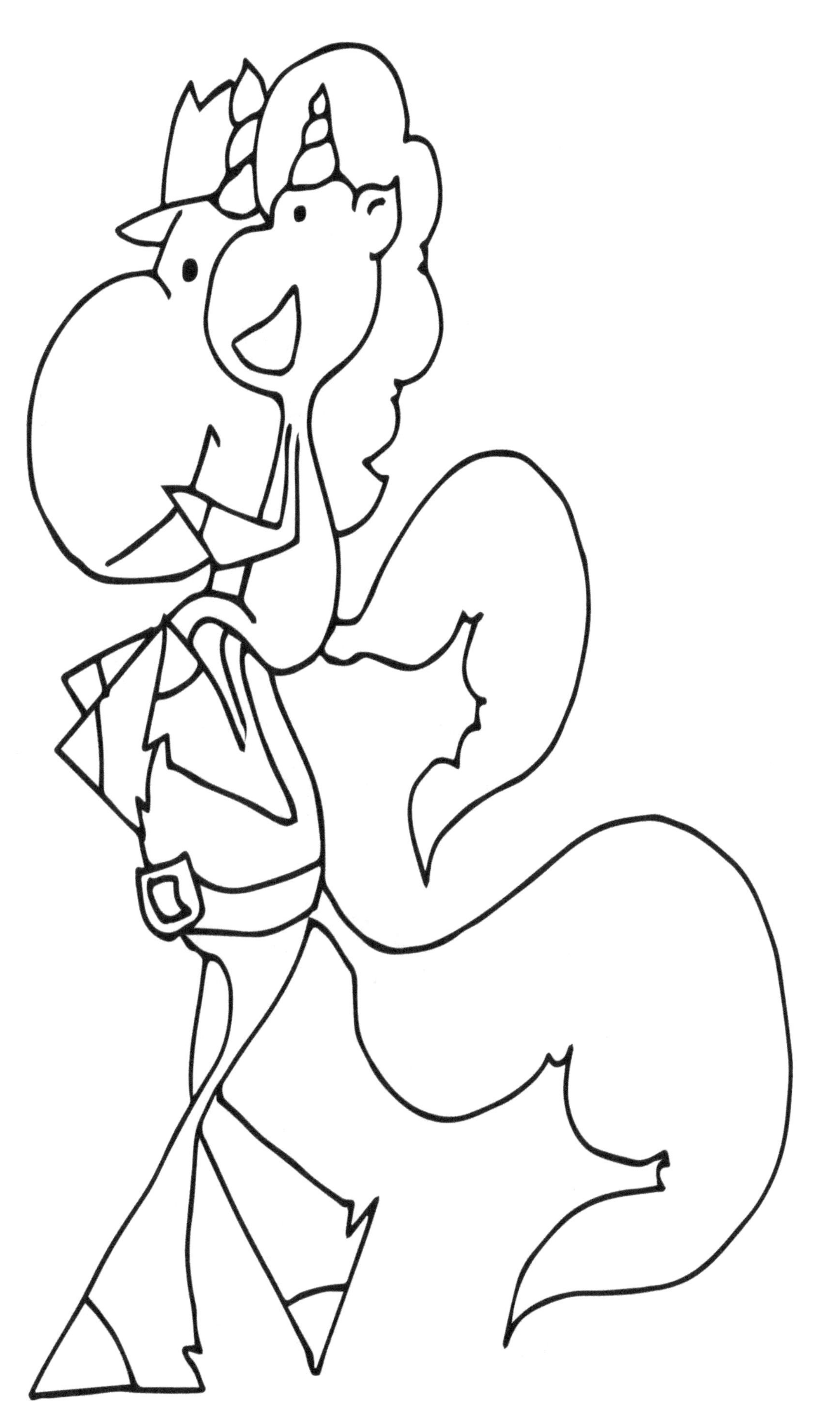

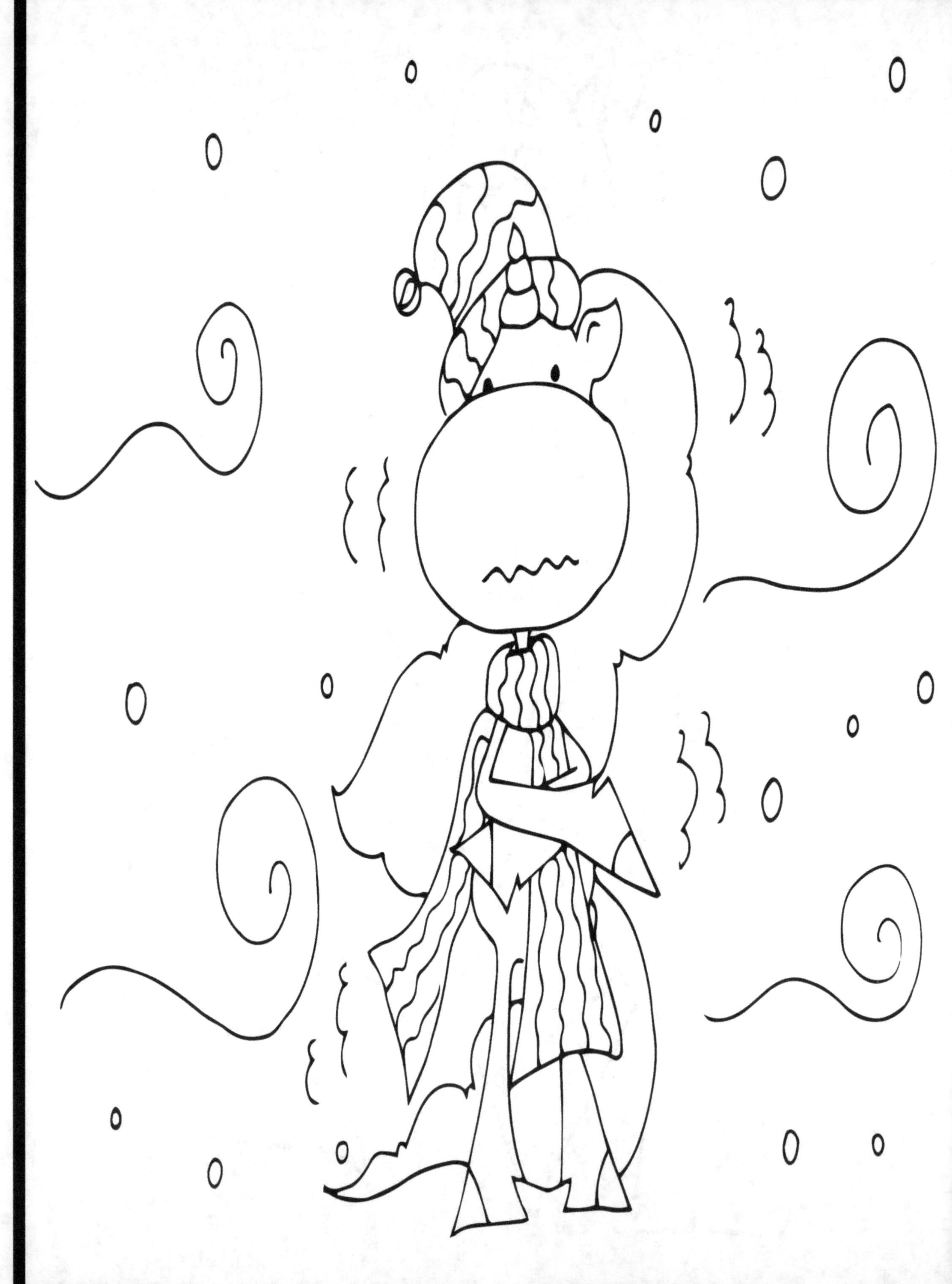

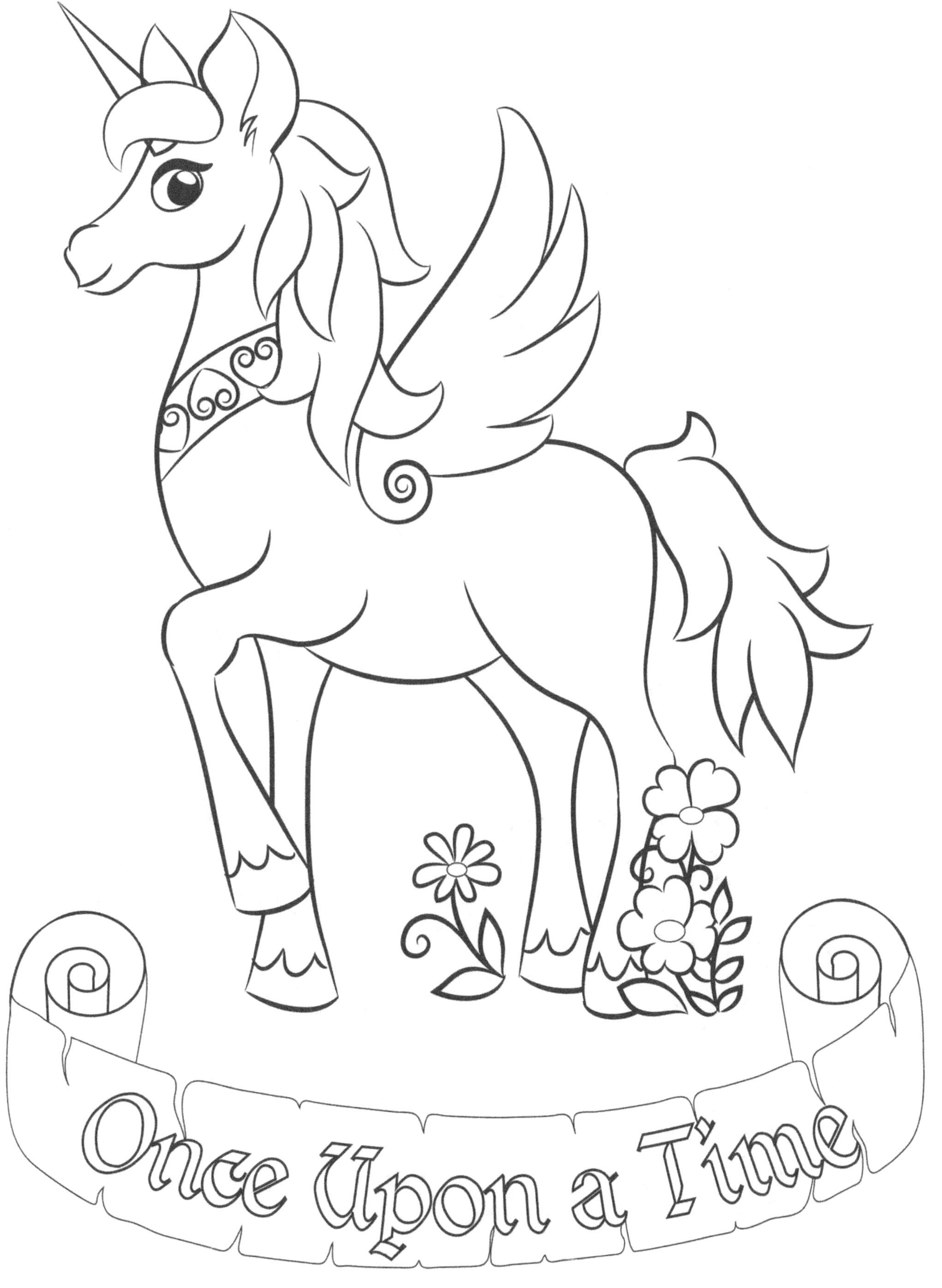
Once Upon a Time

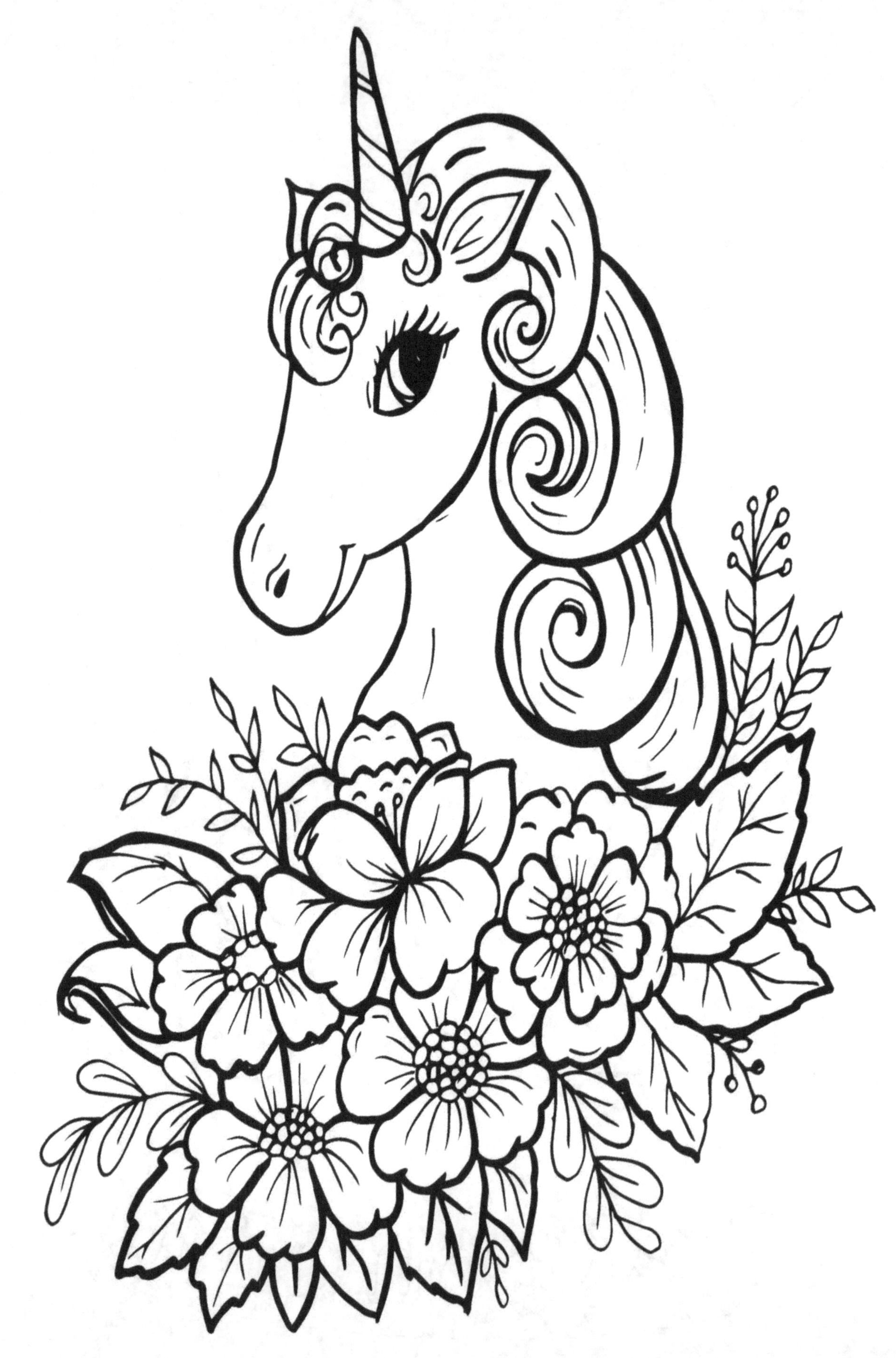

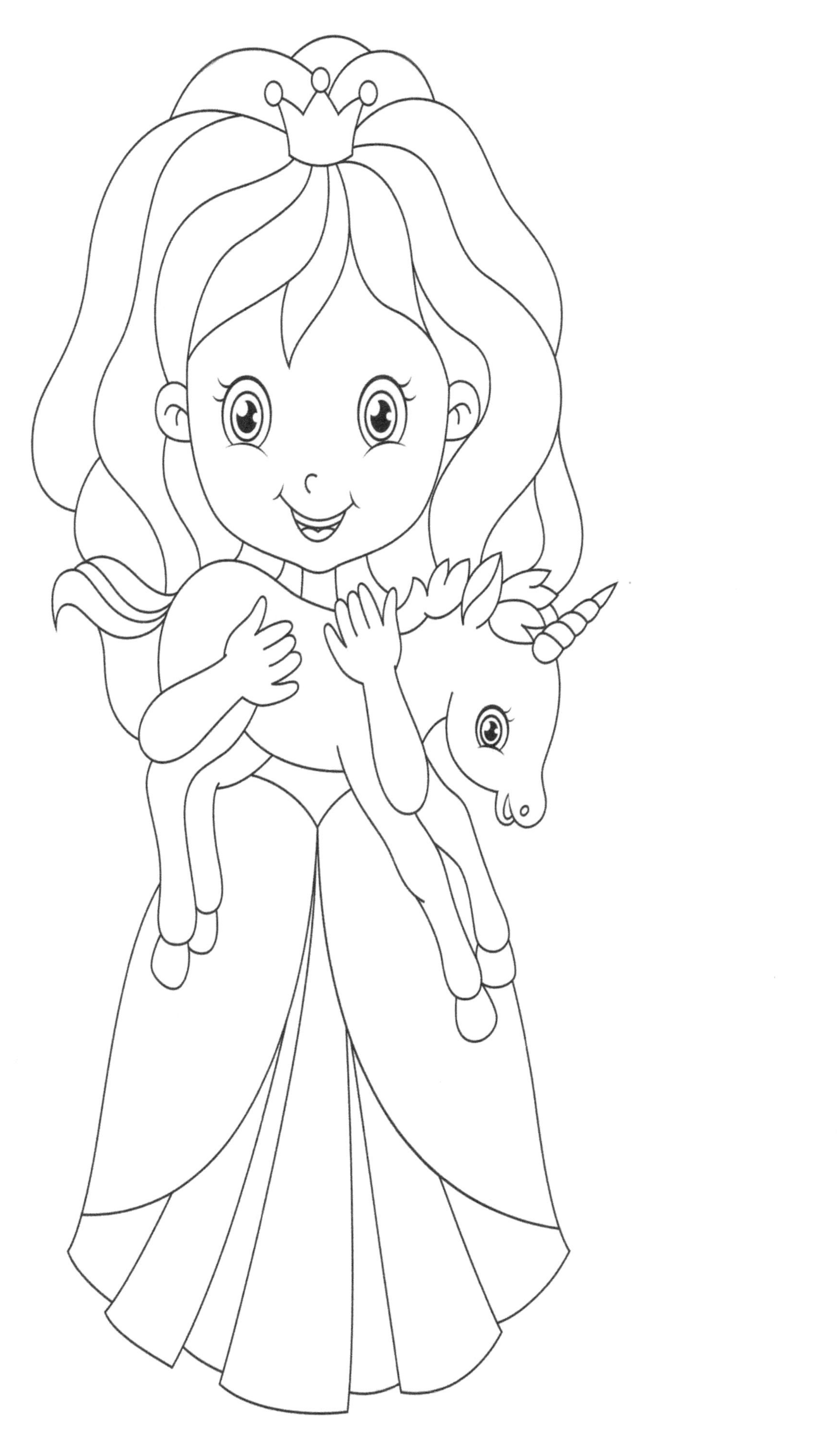

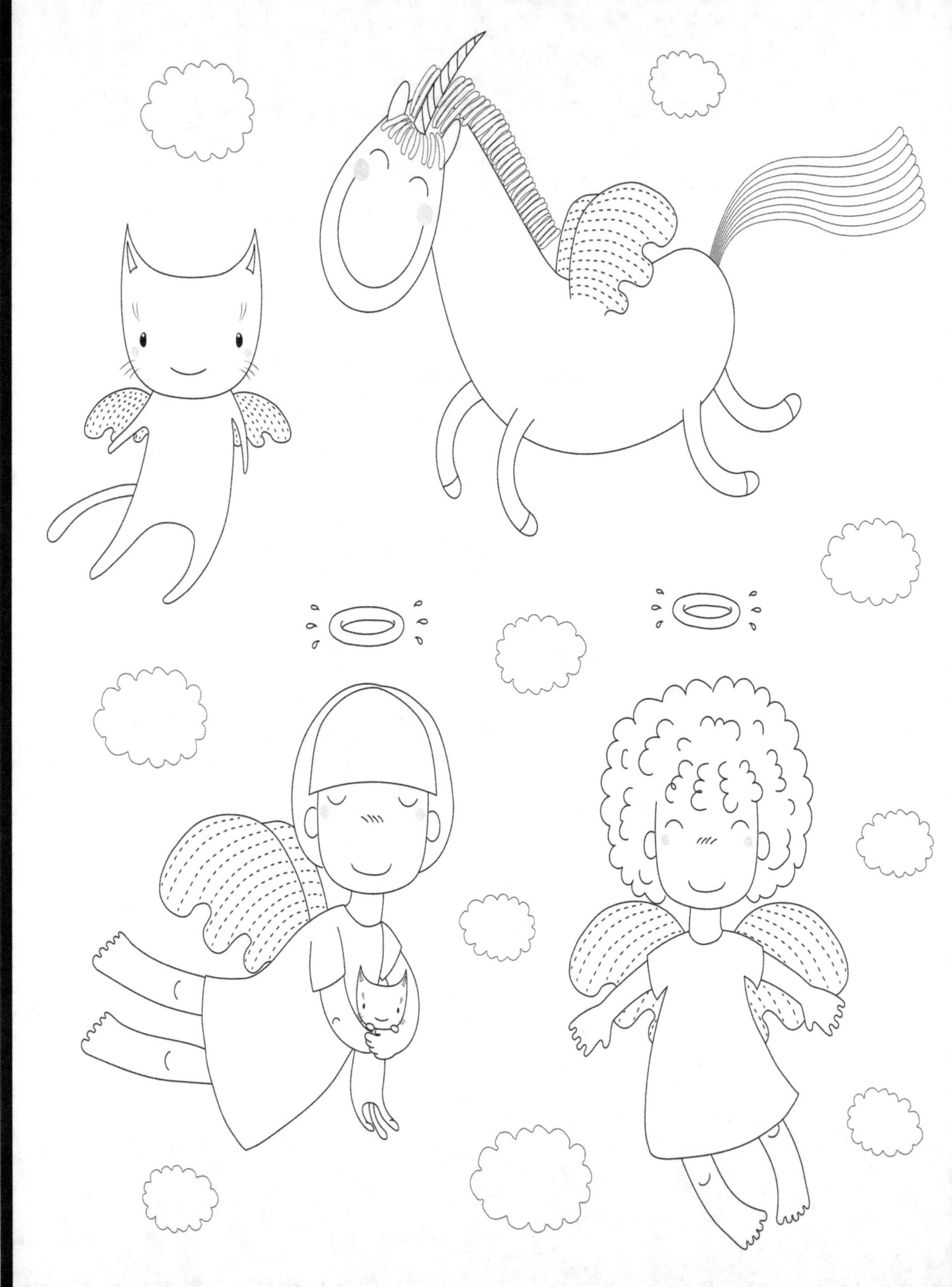

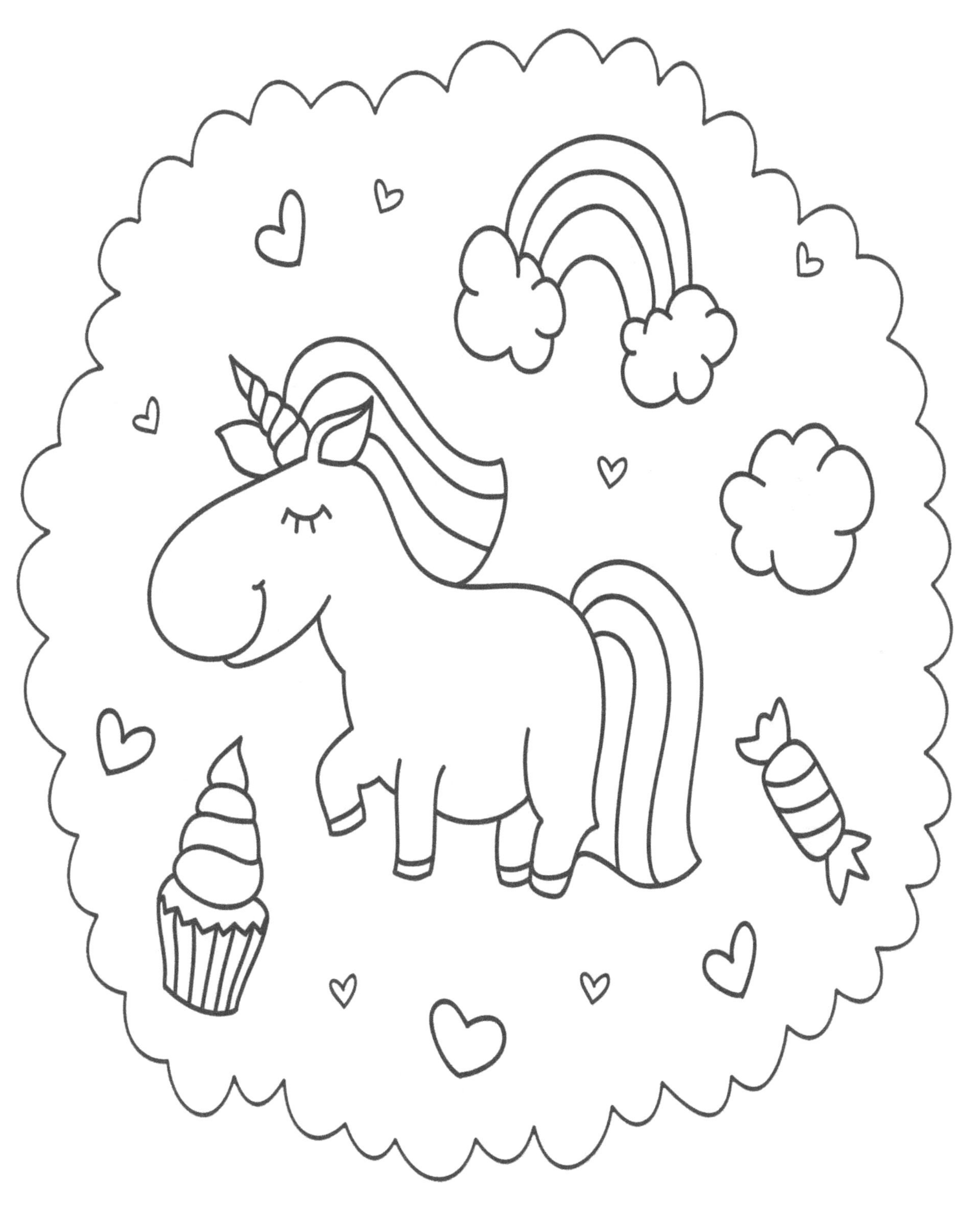

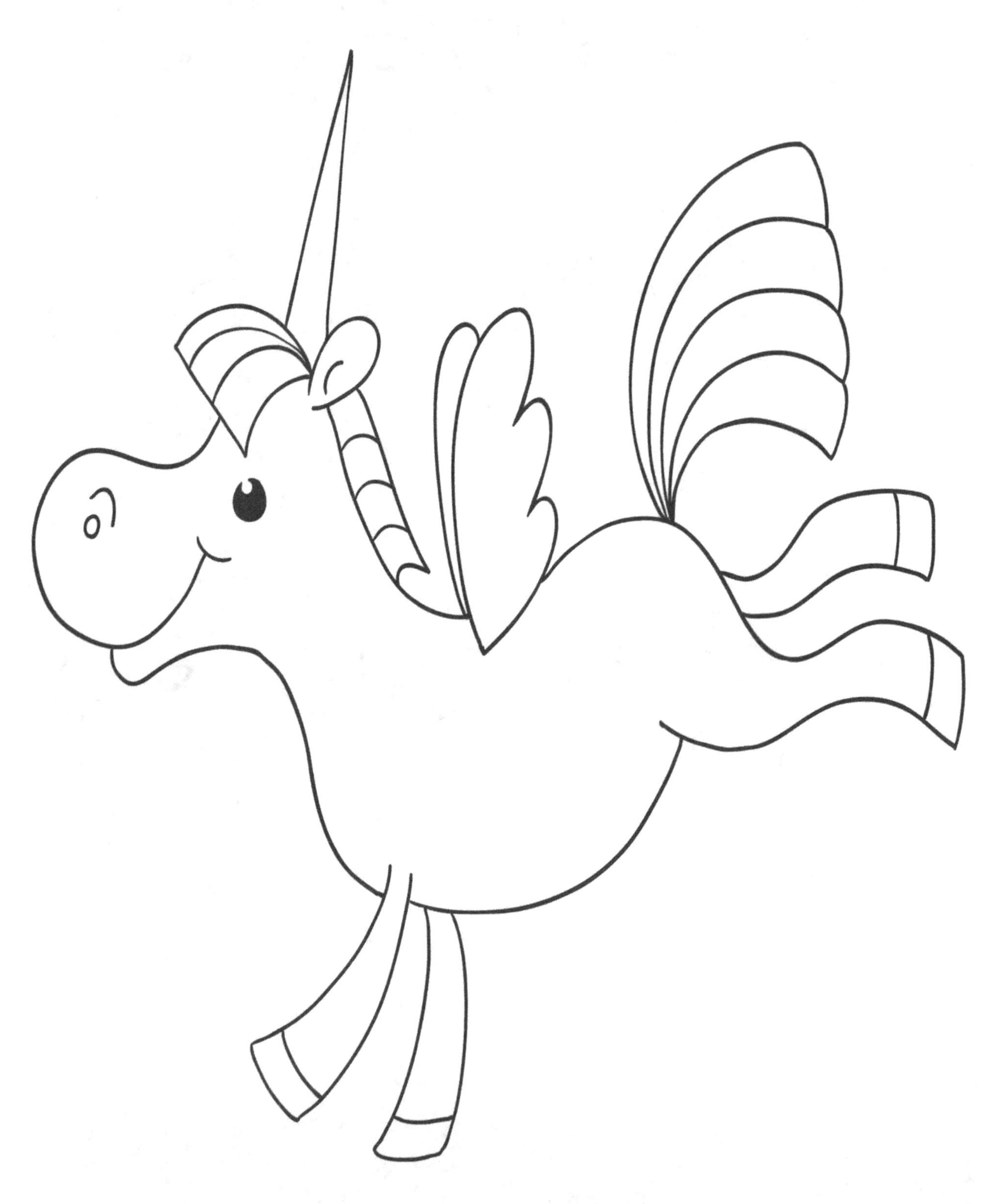

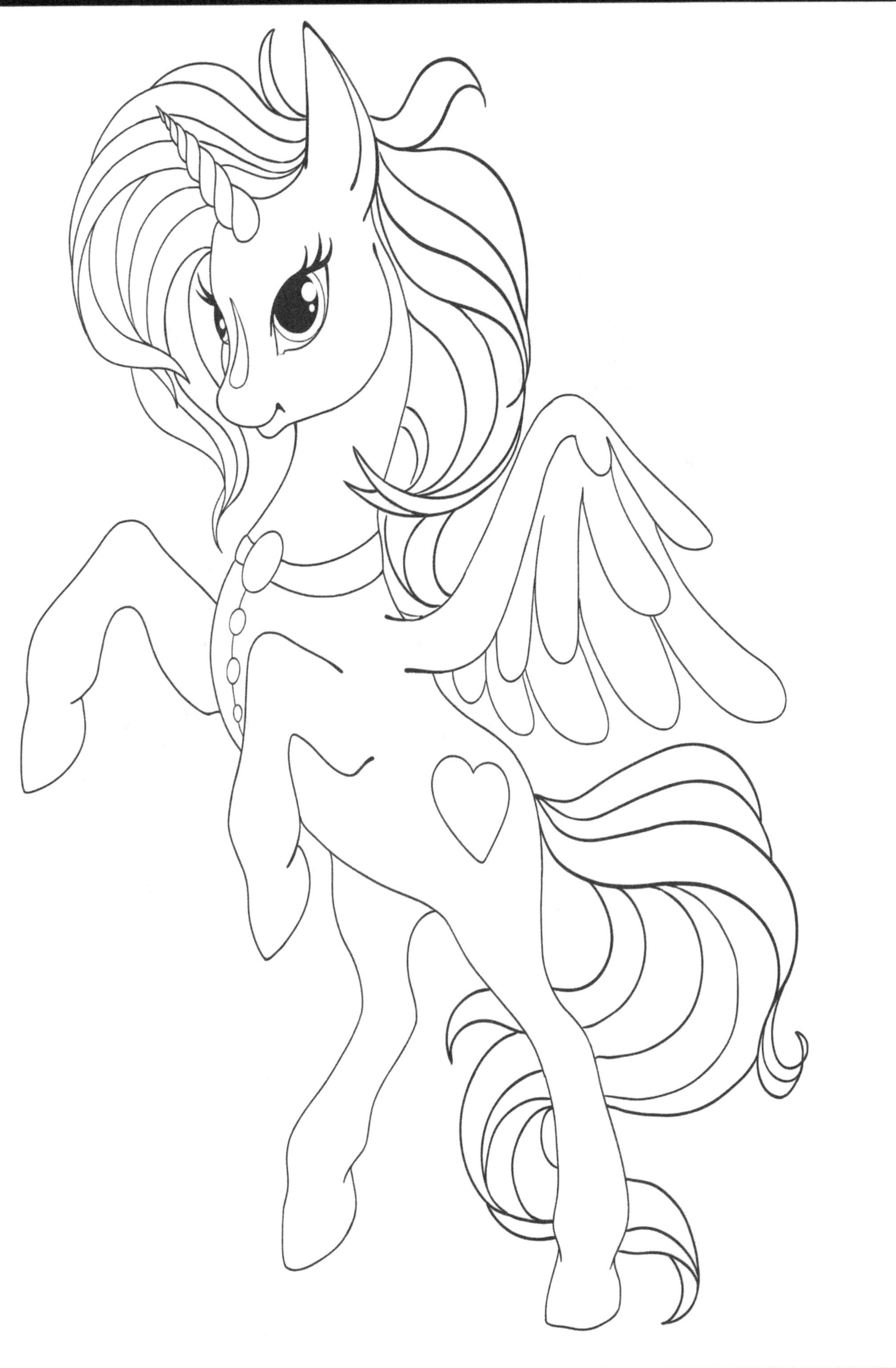

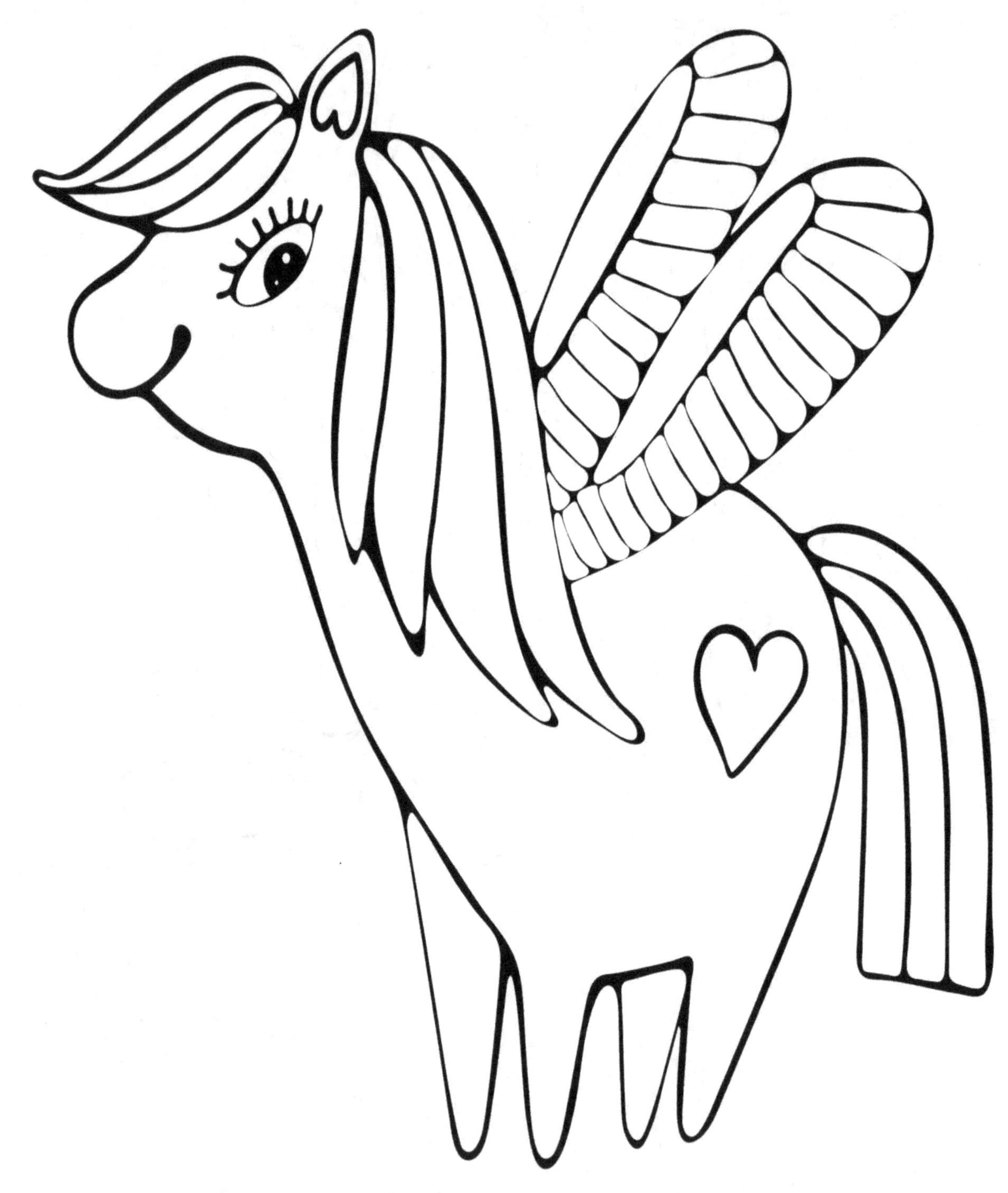

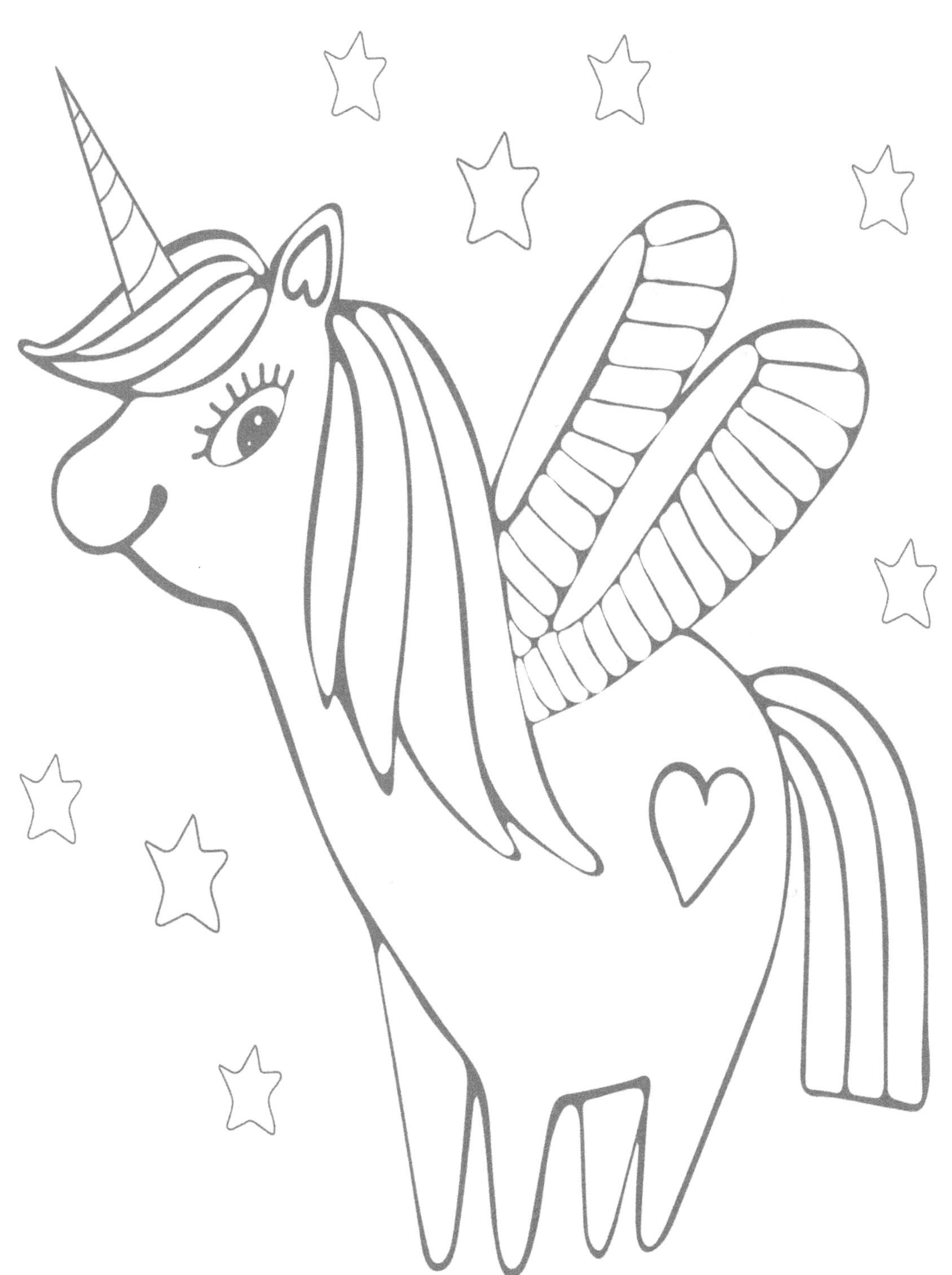

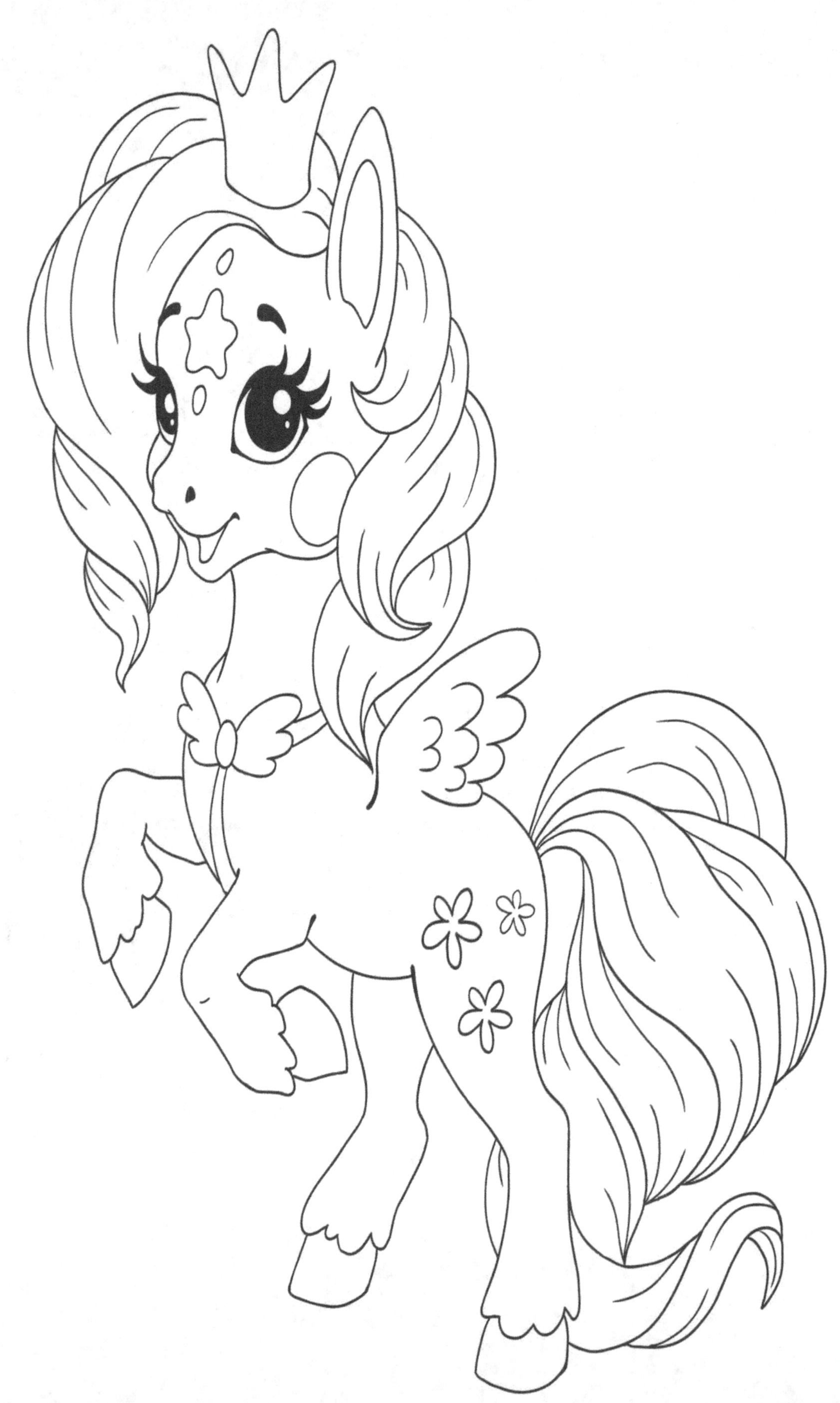

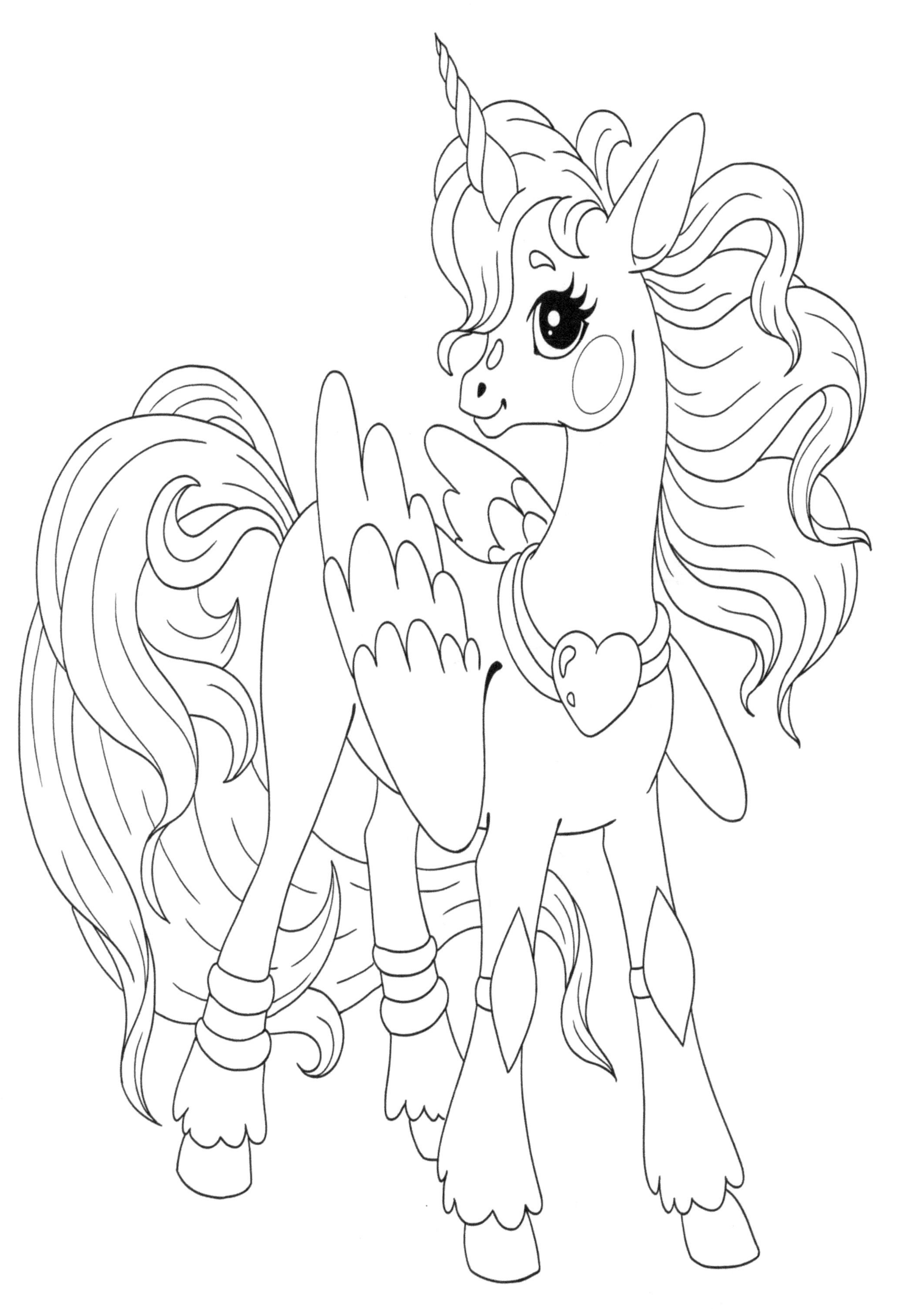

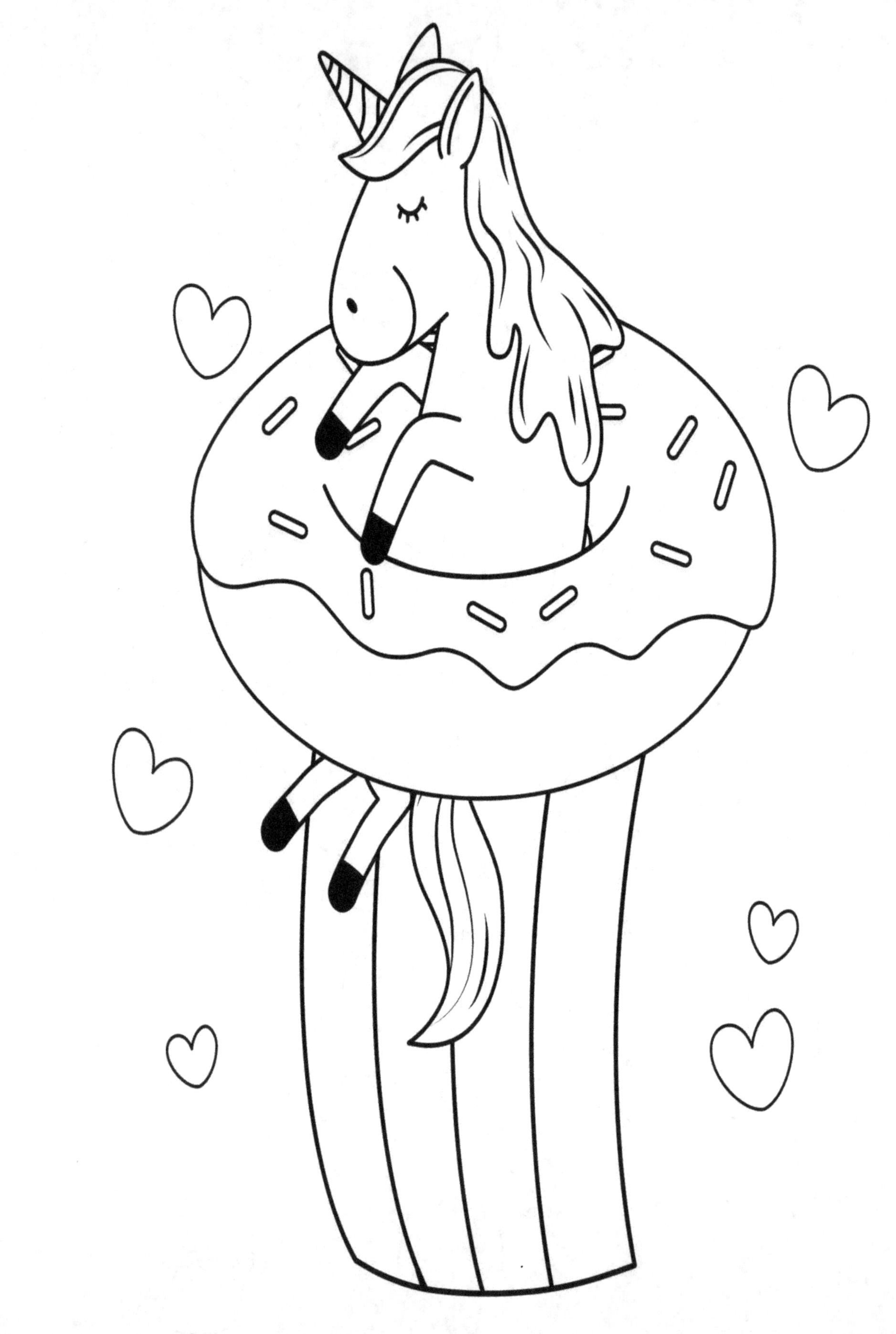

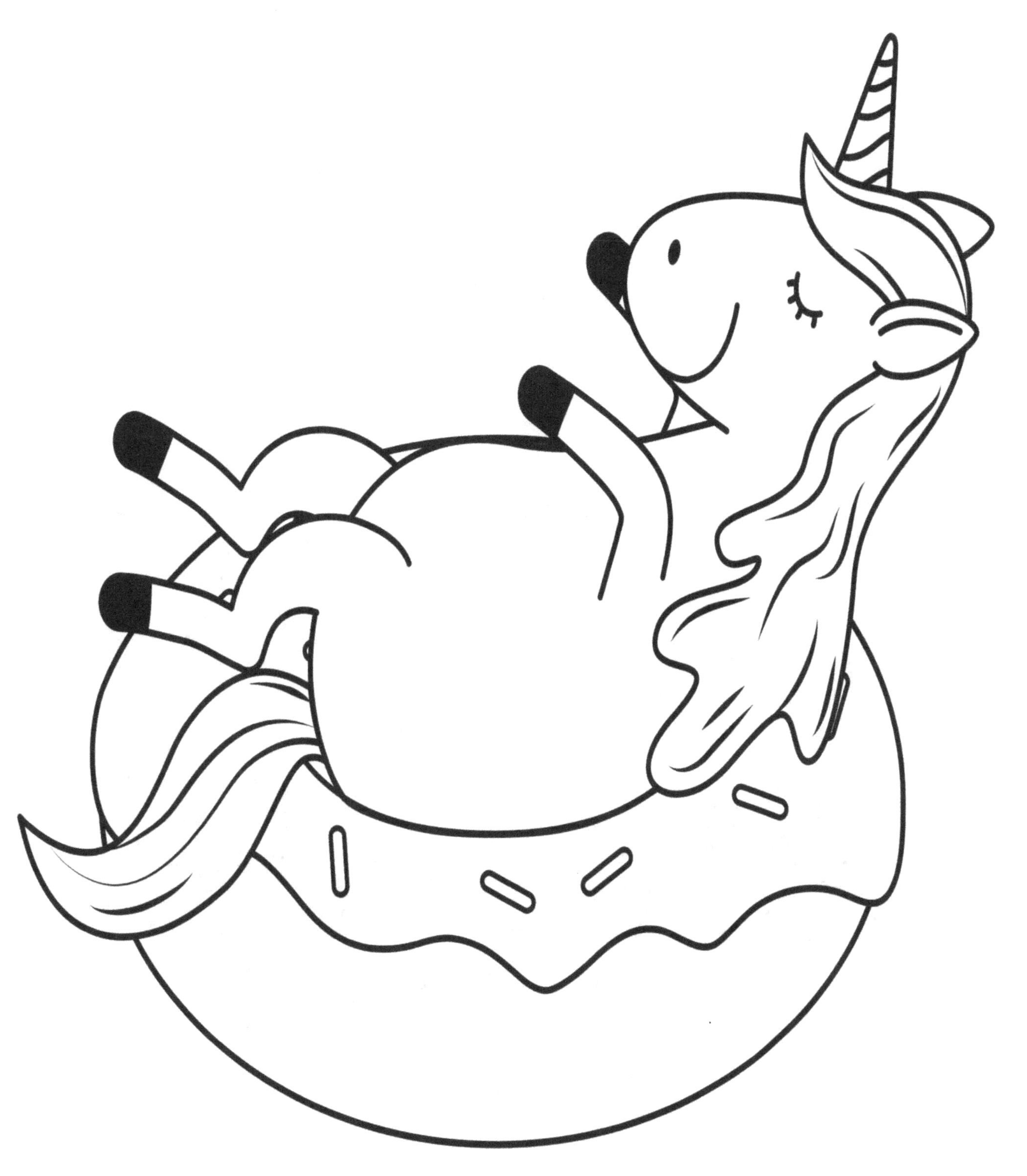

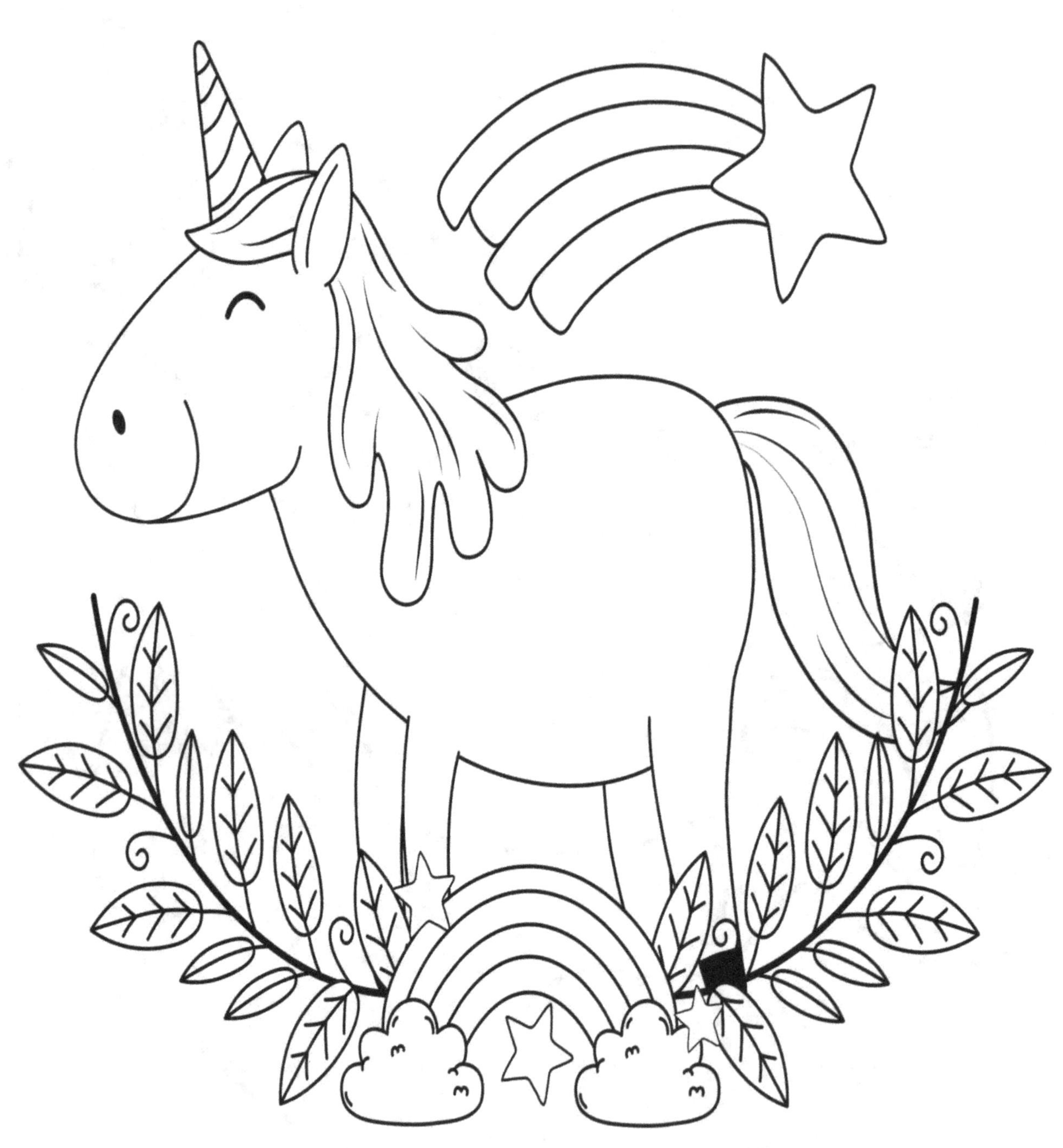

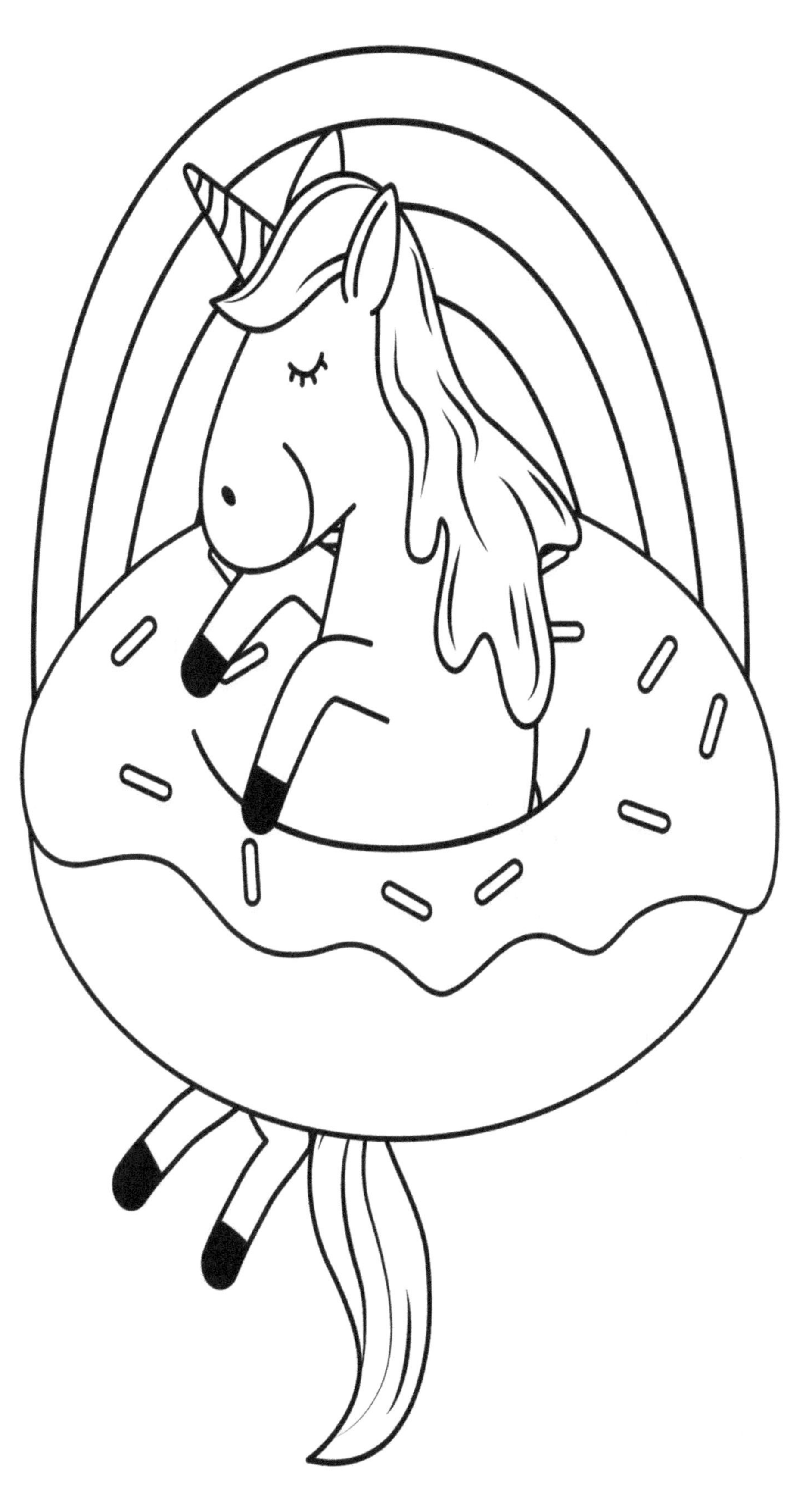

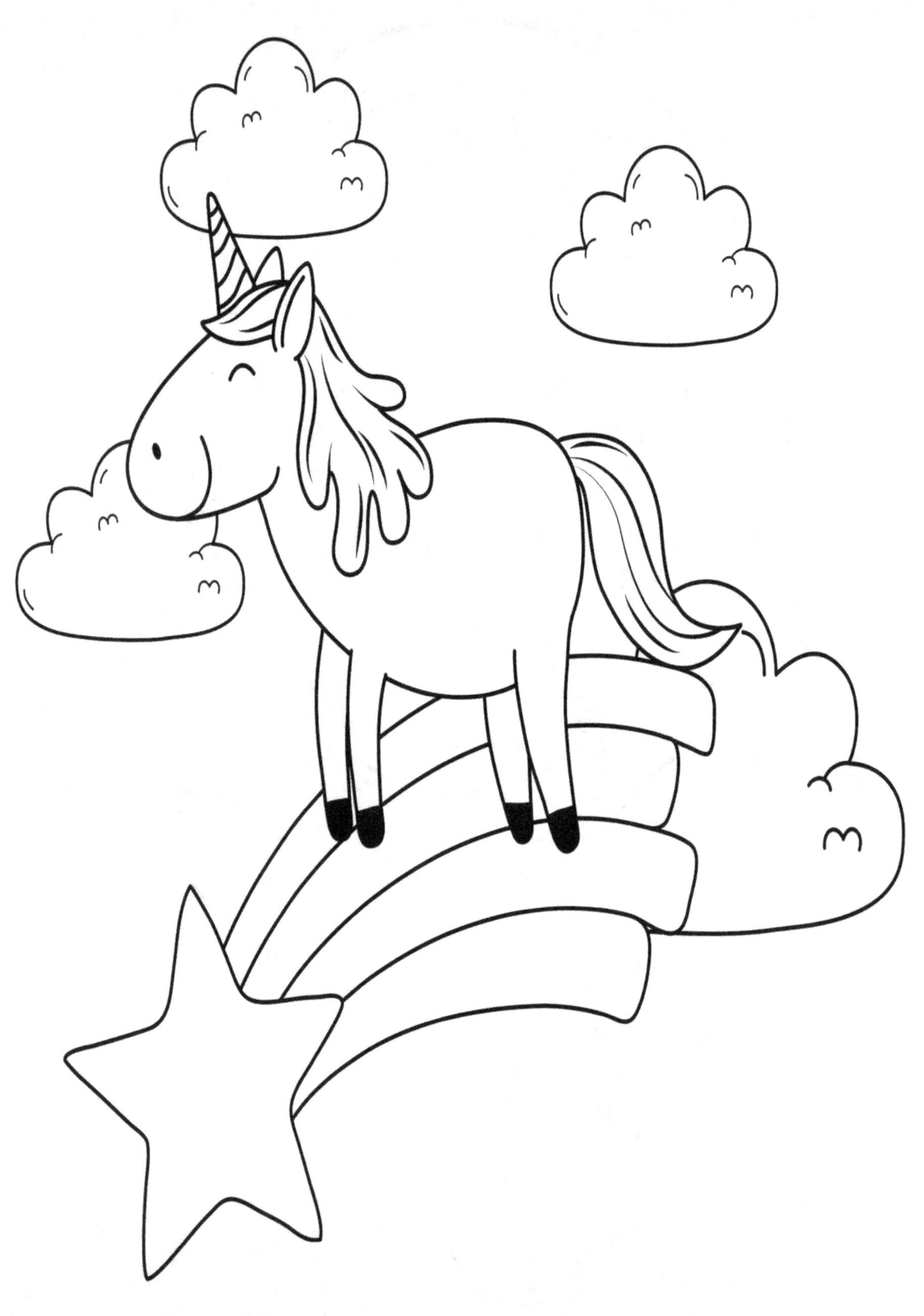

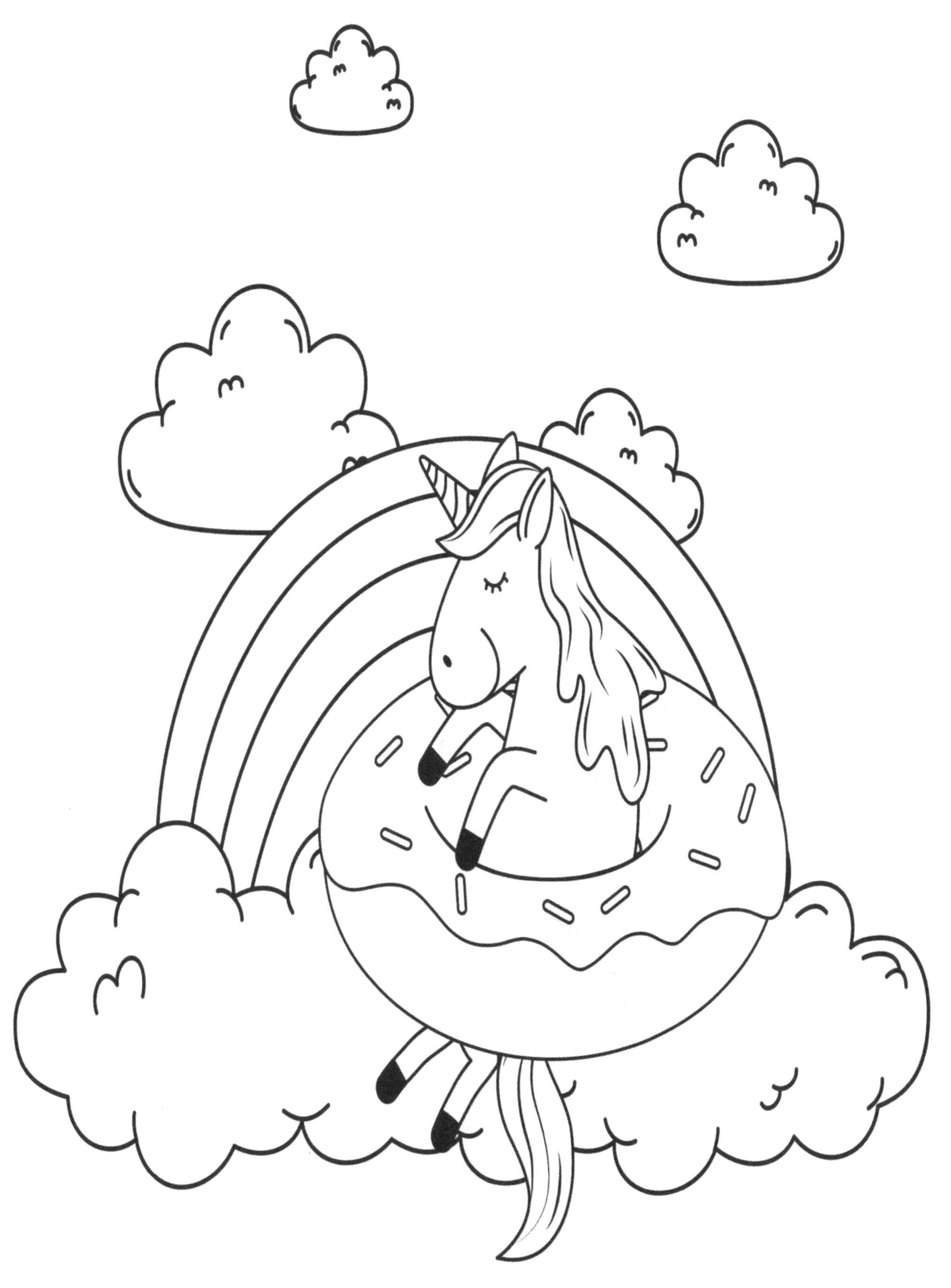

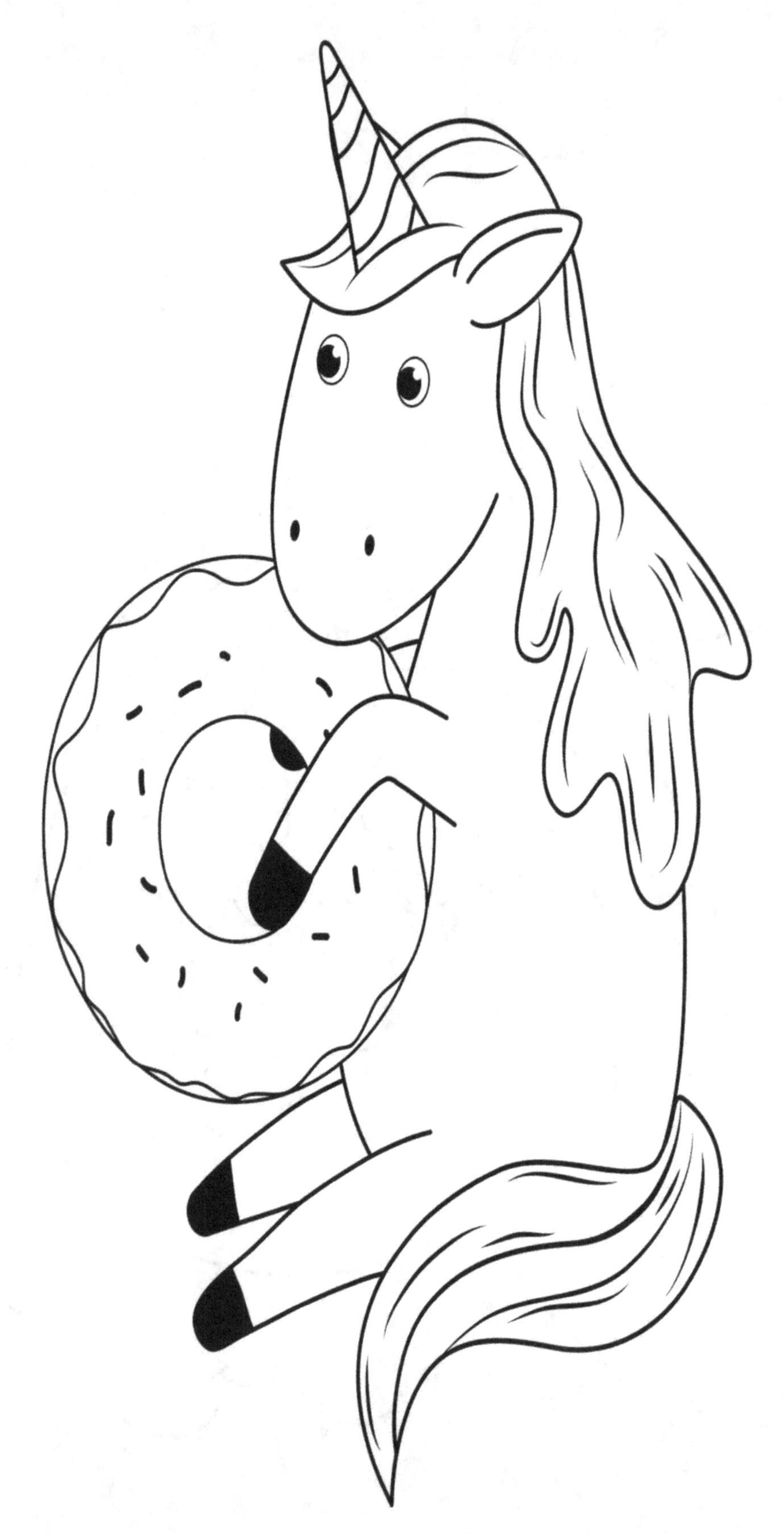

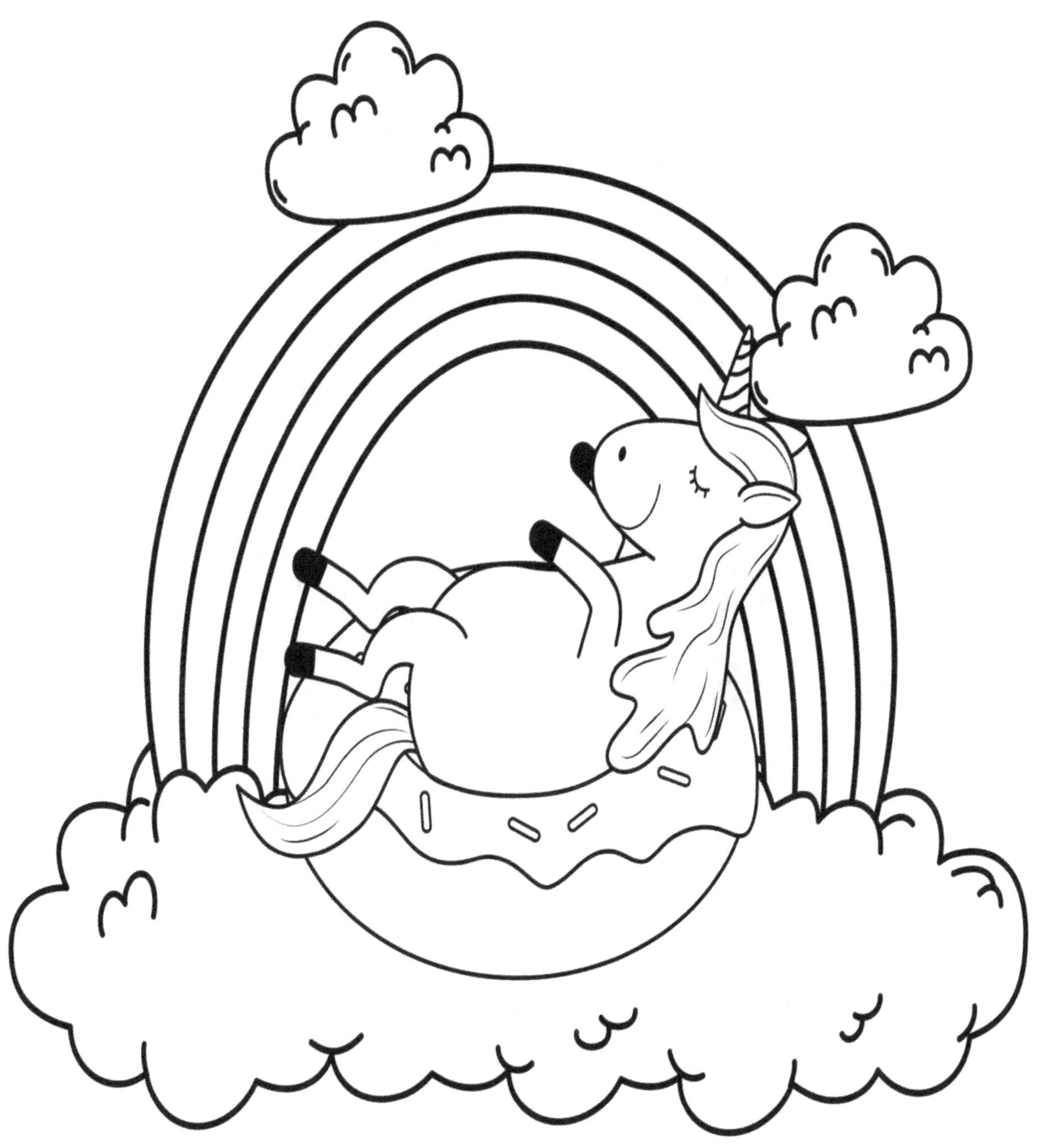

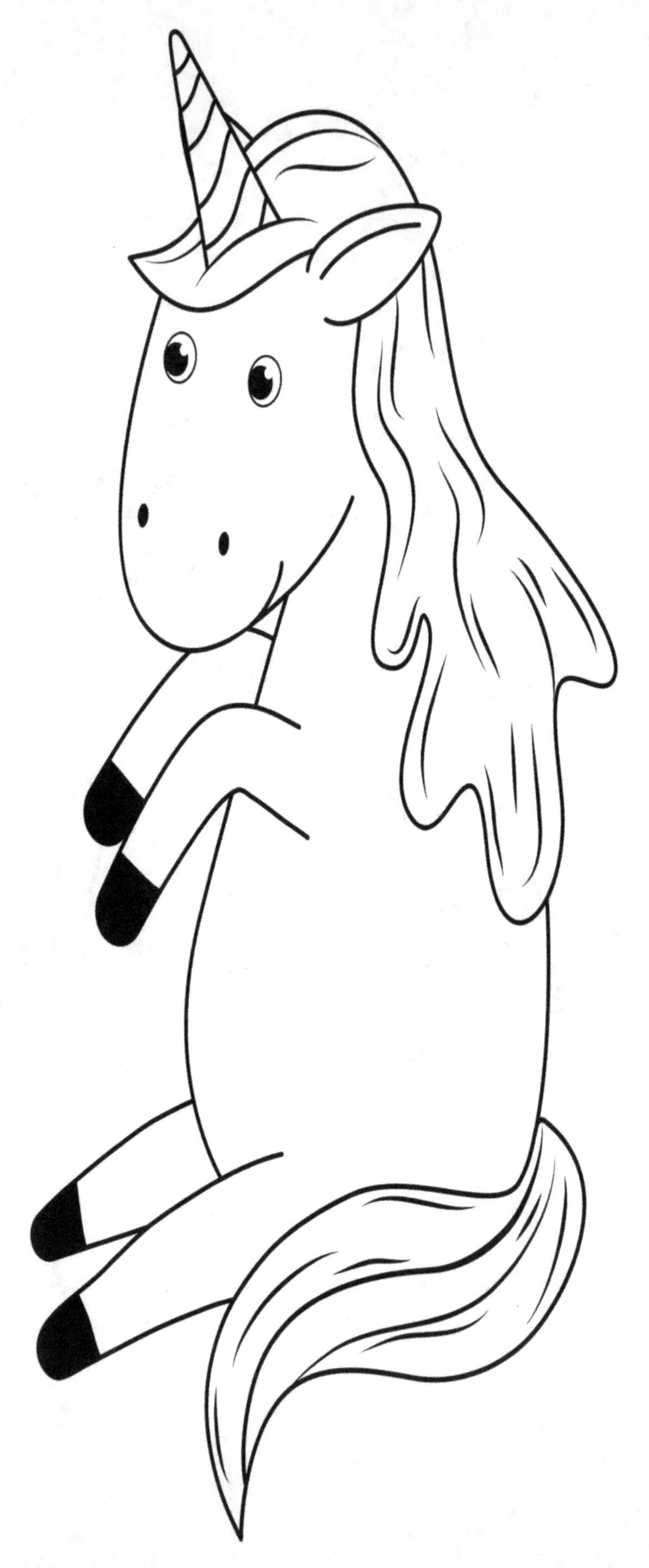

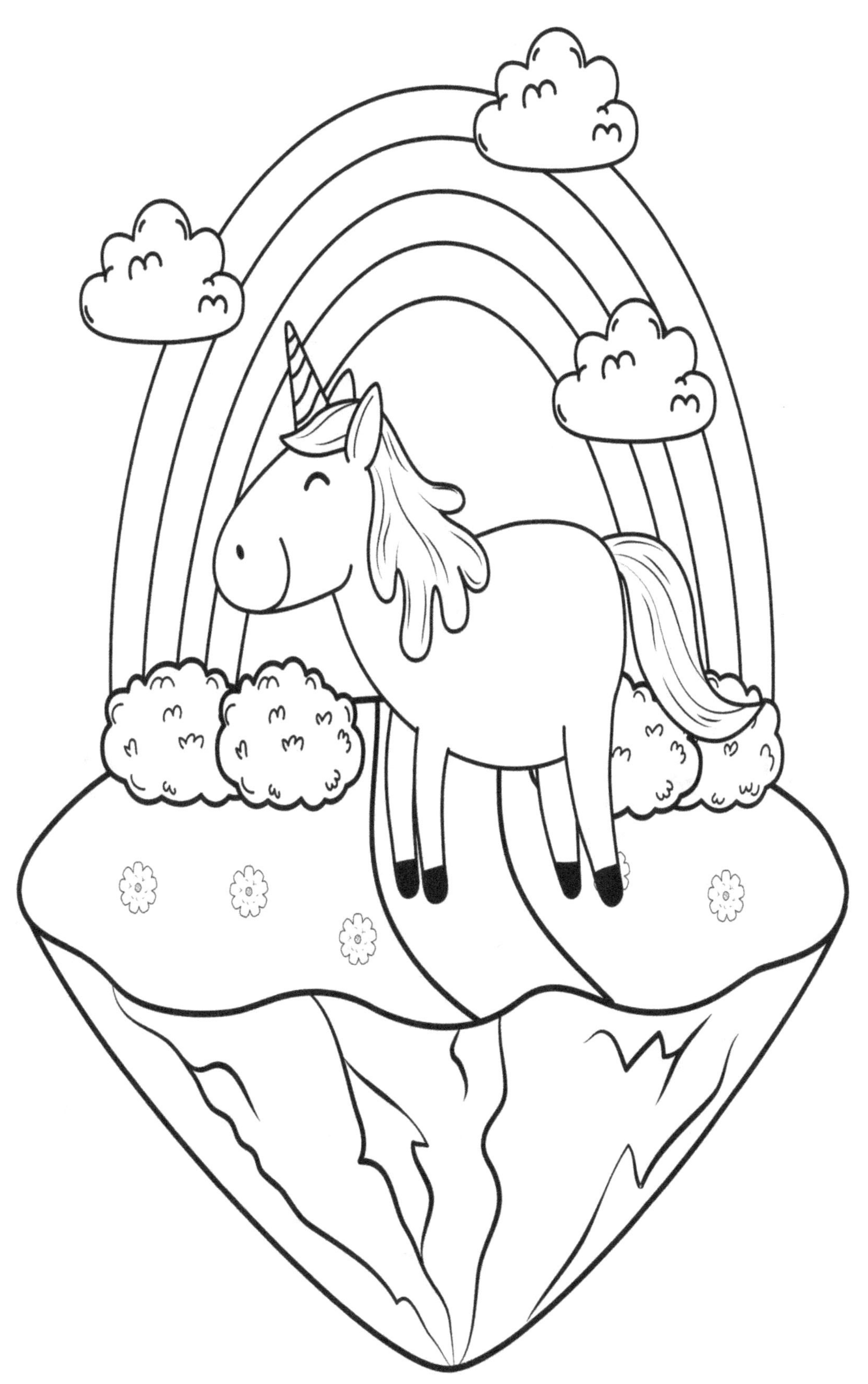

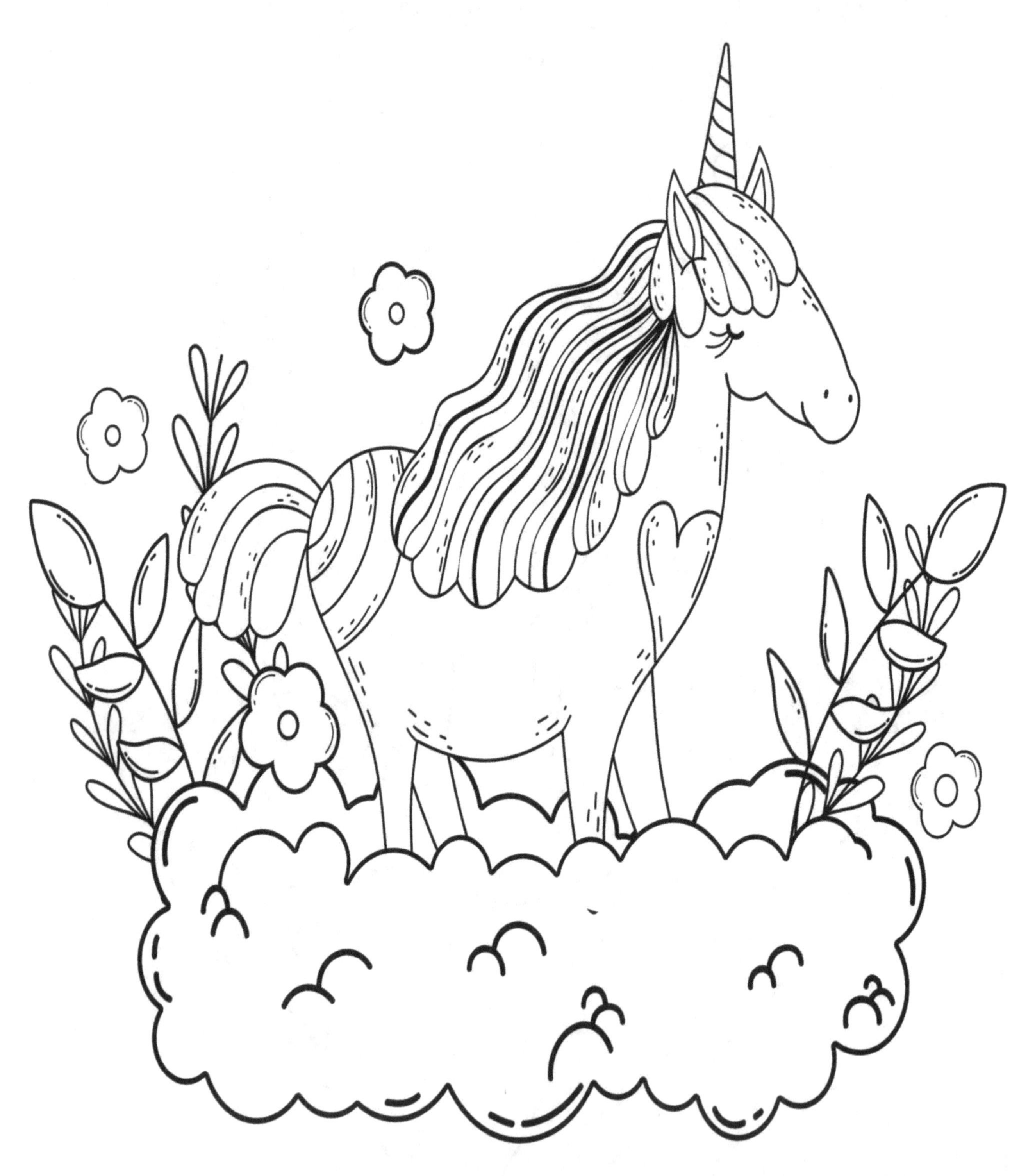

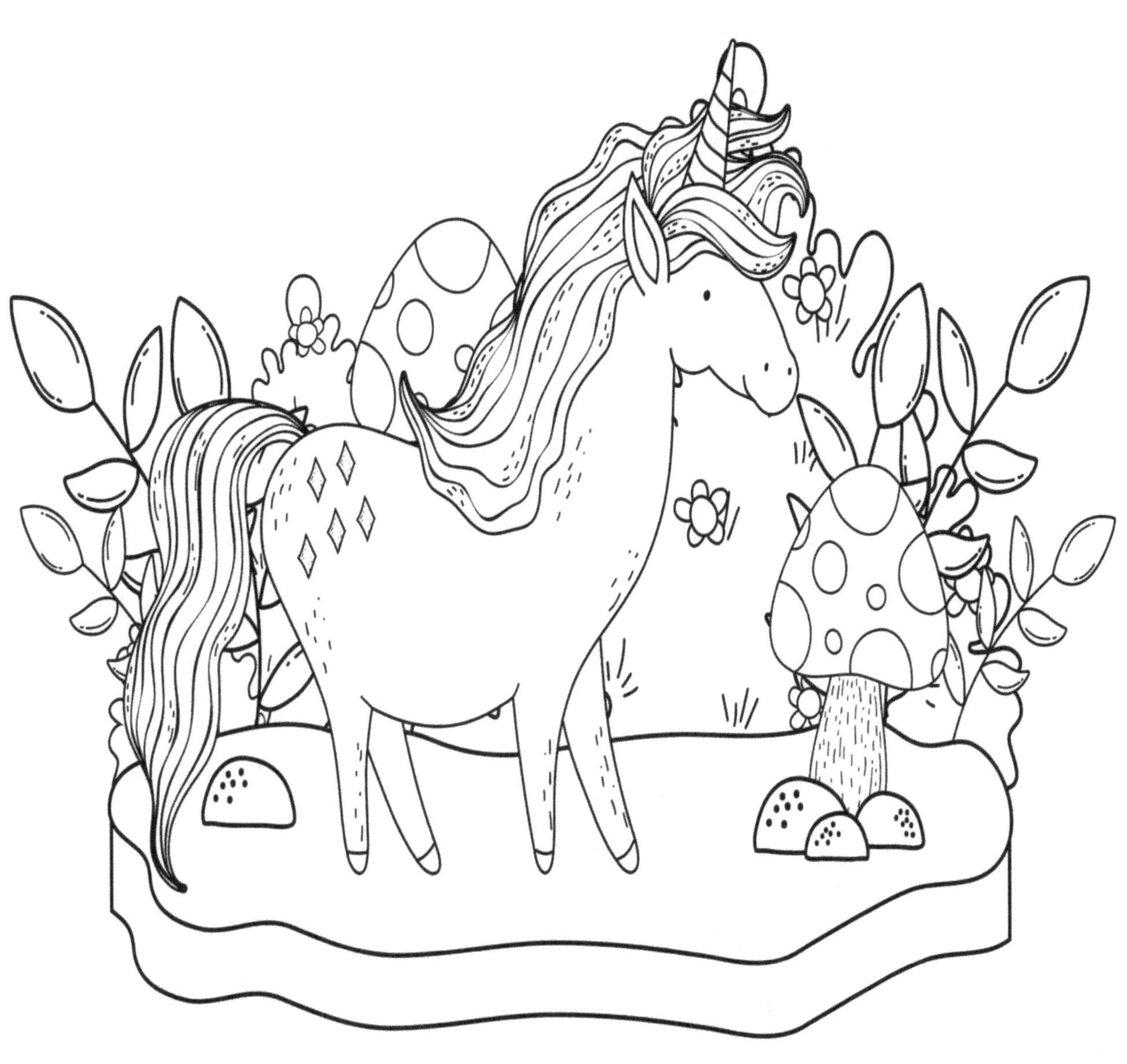

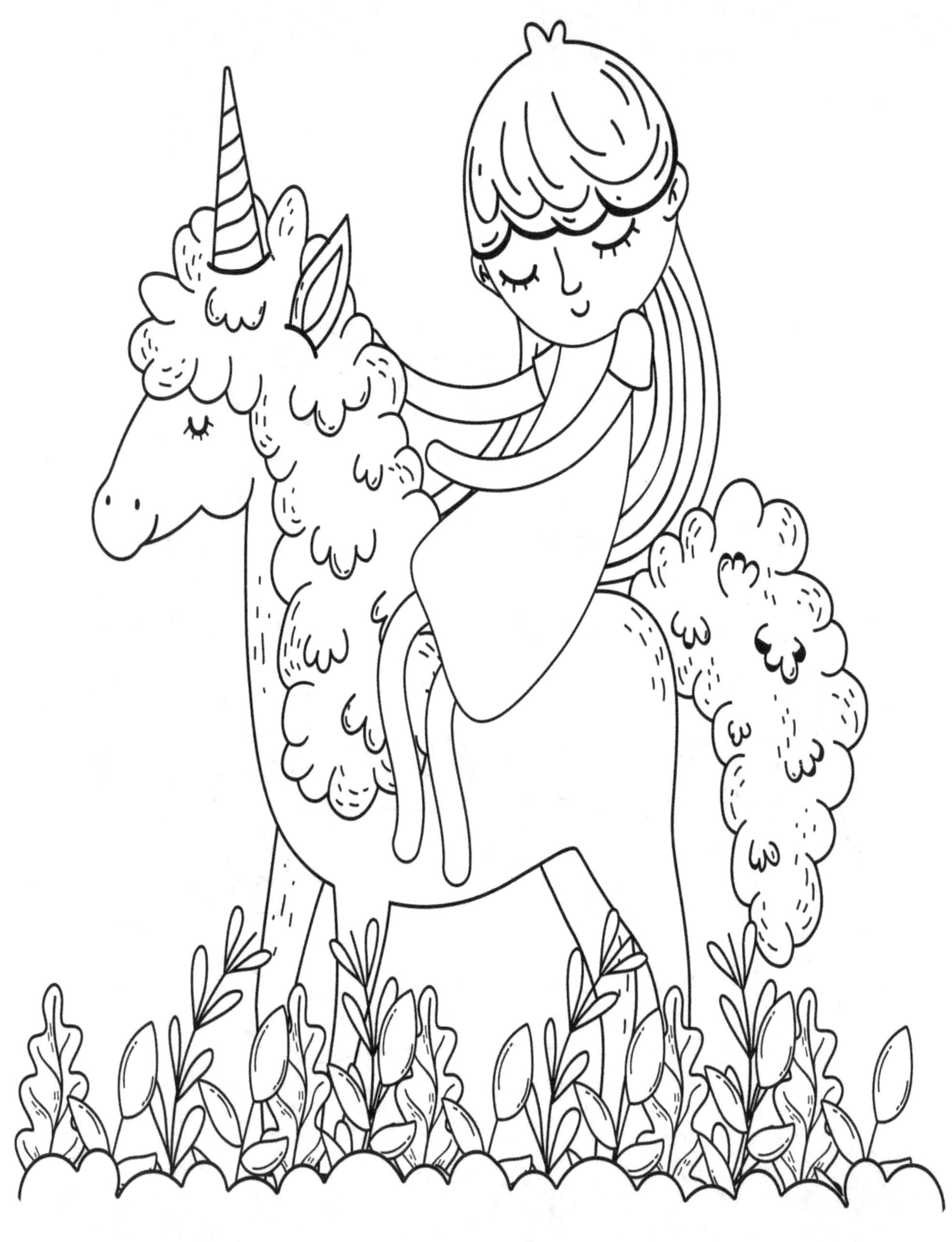

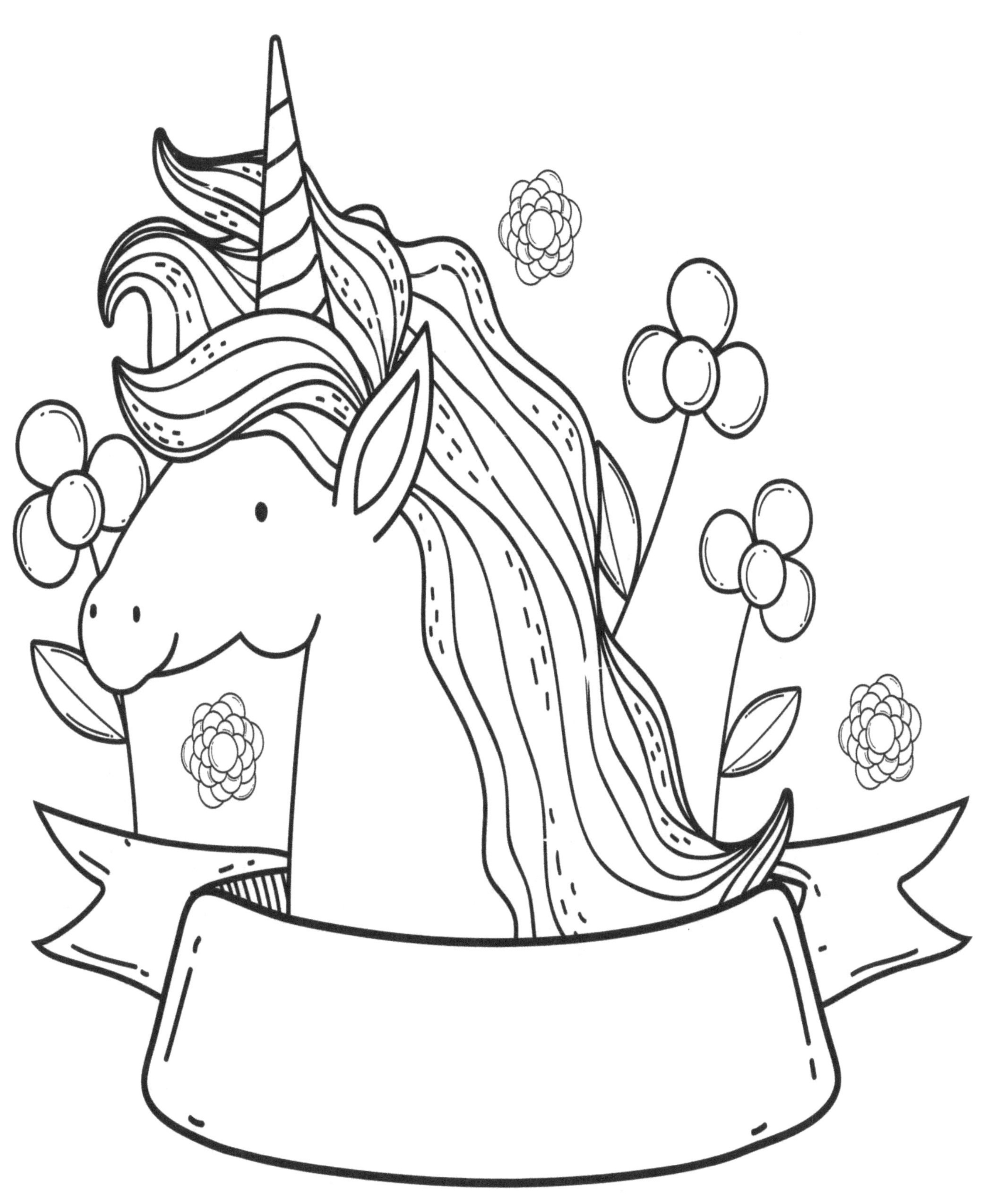

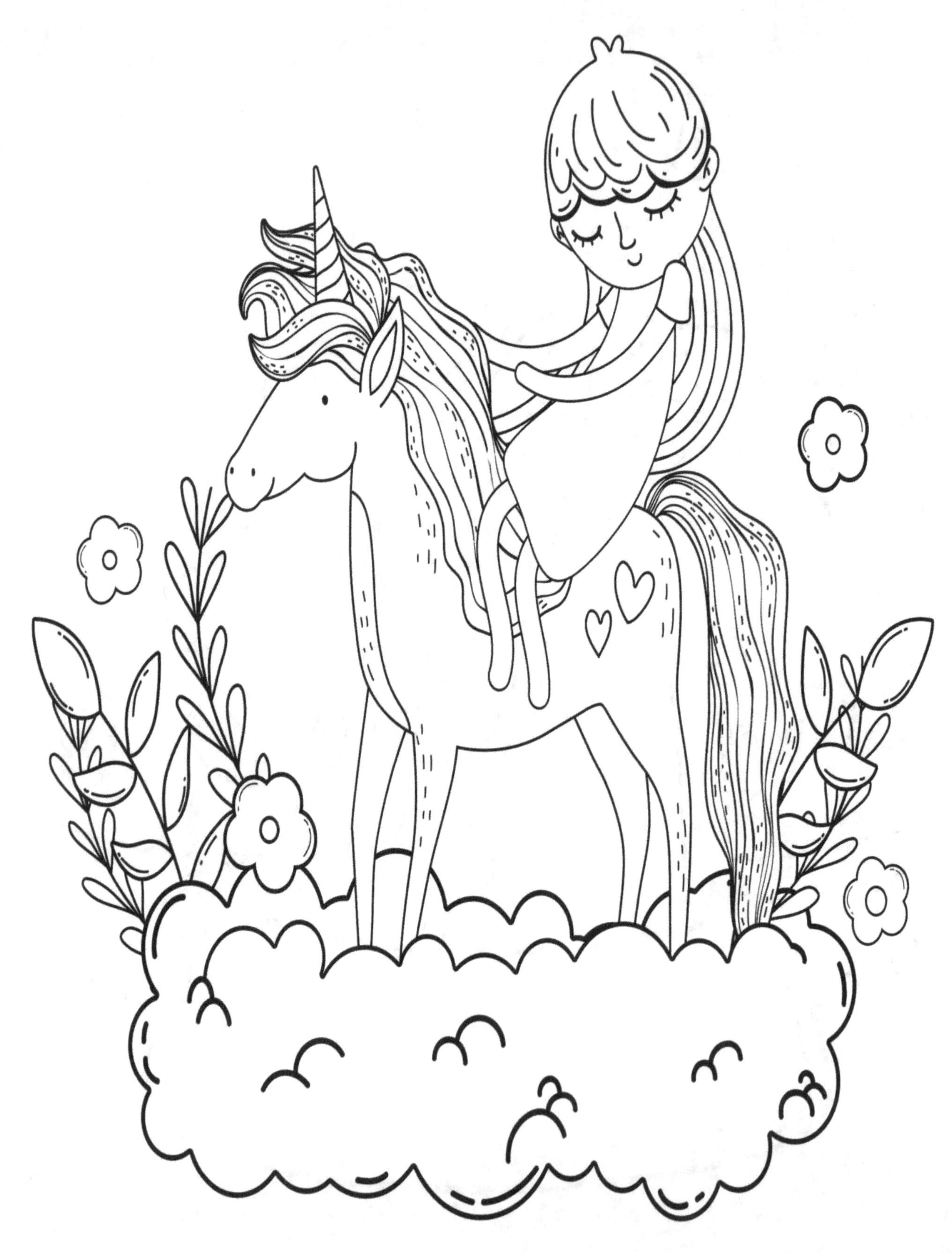

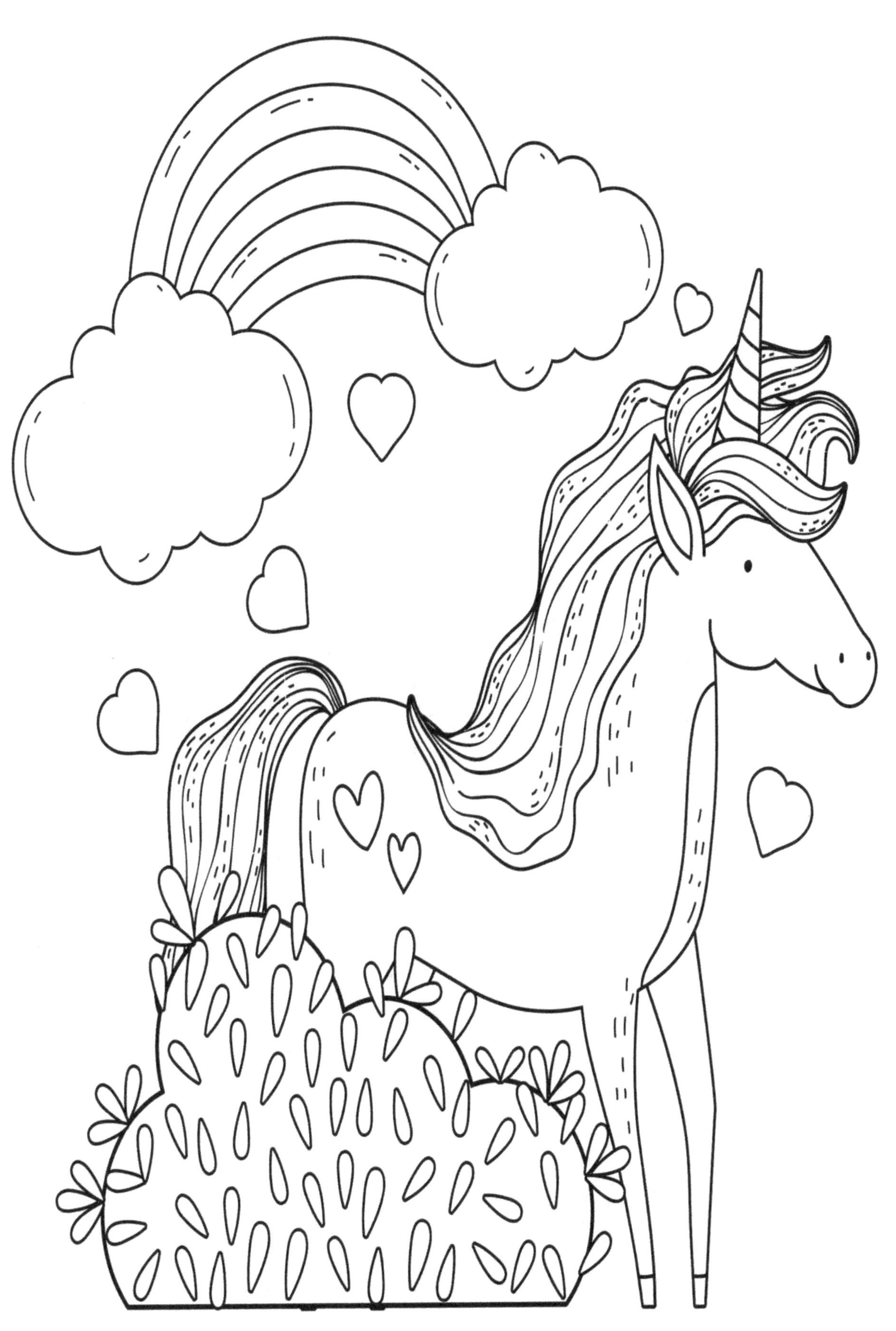

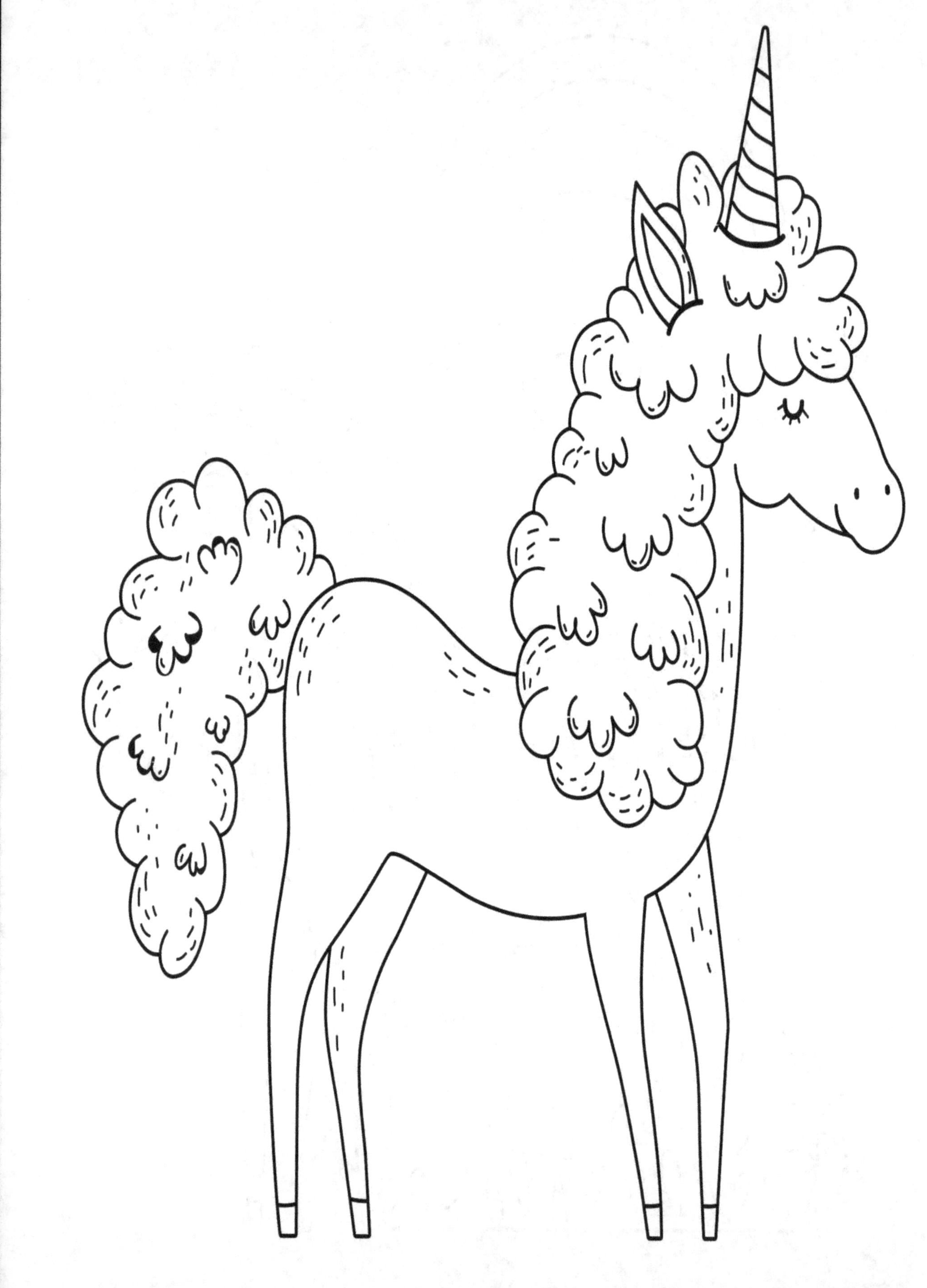

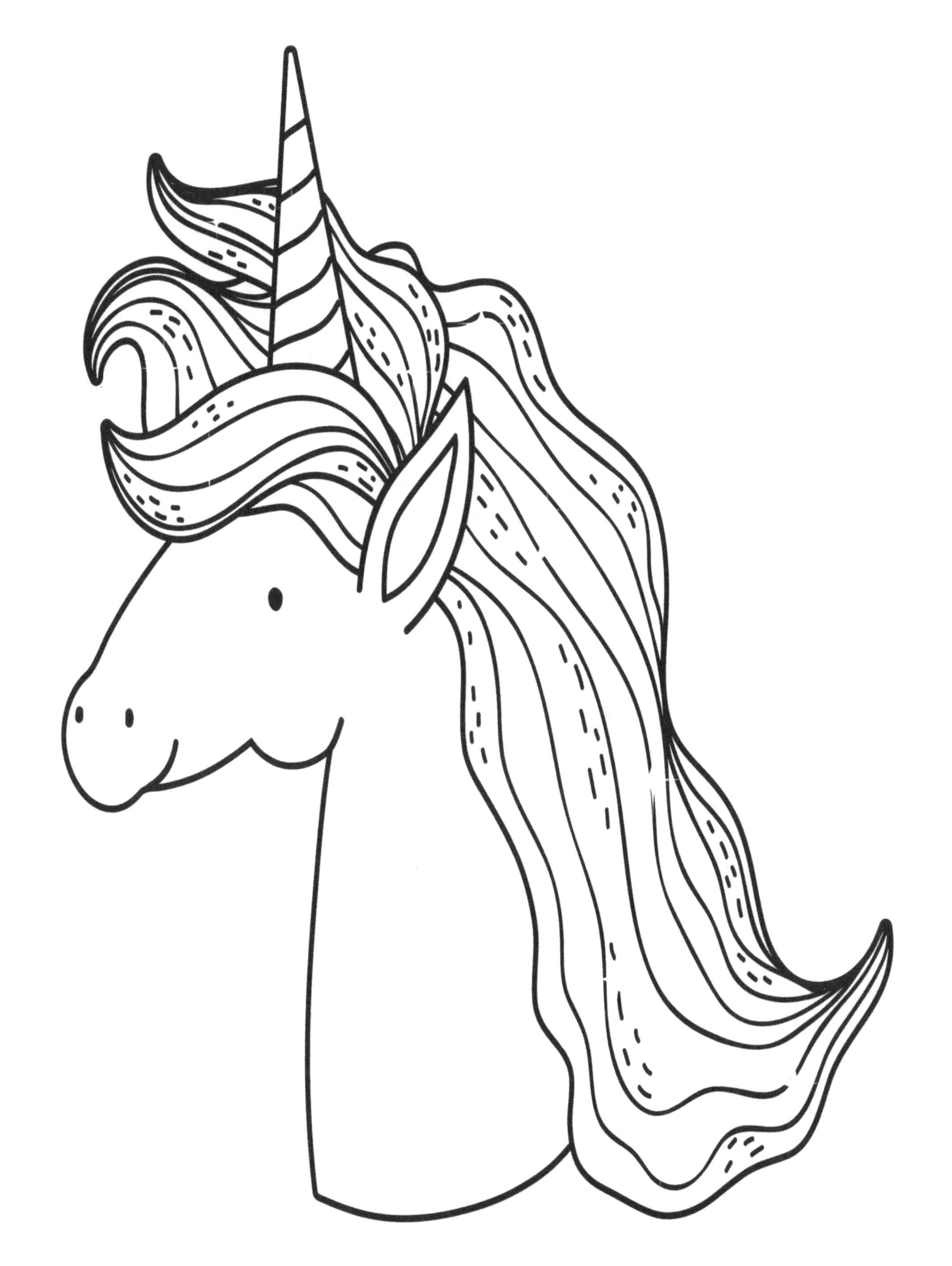

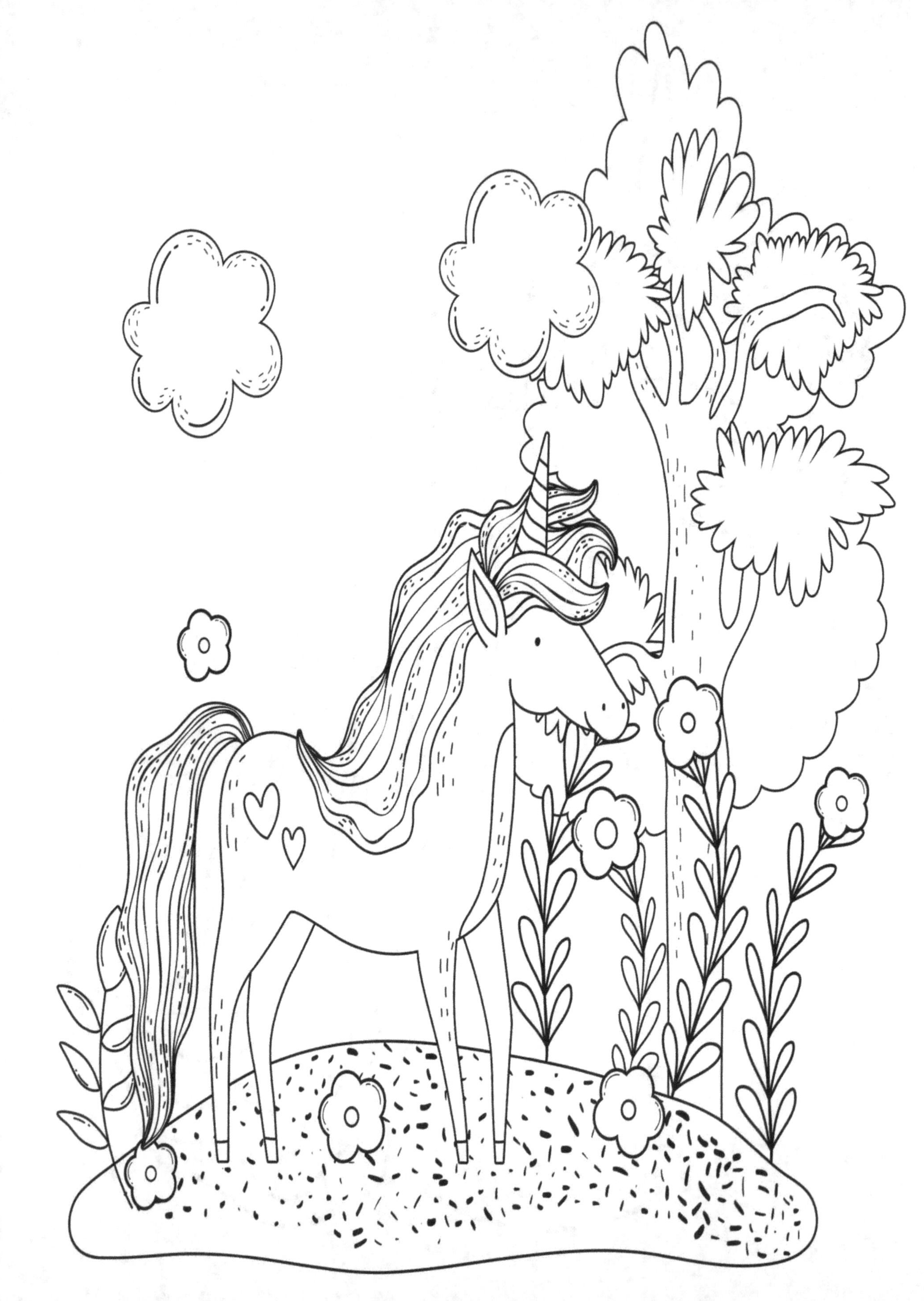

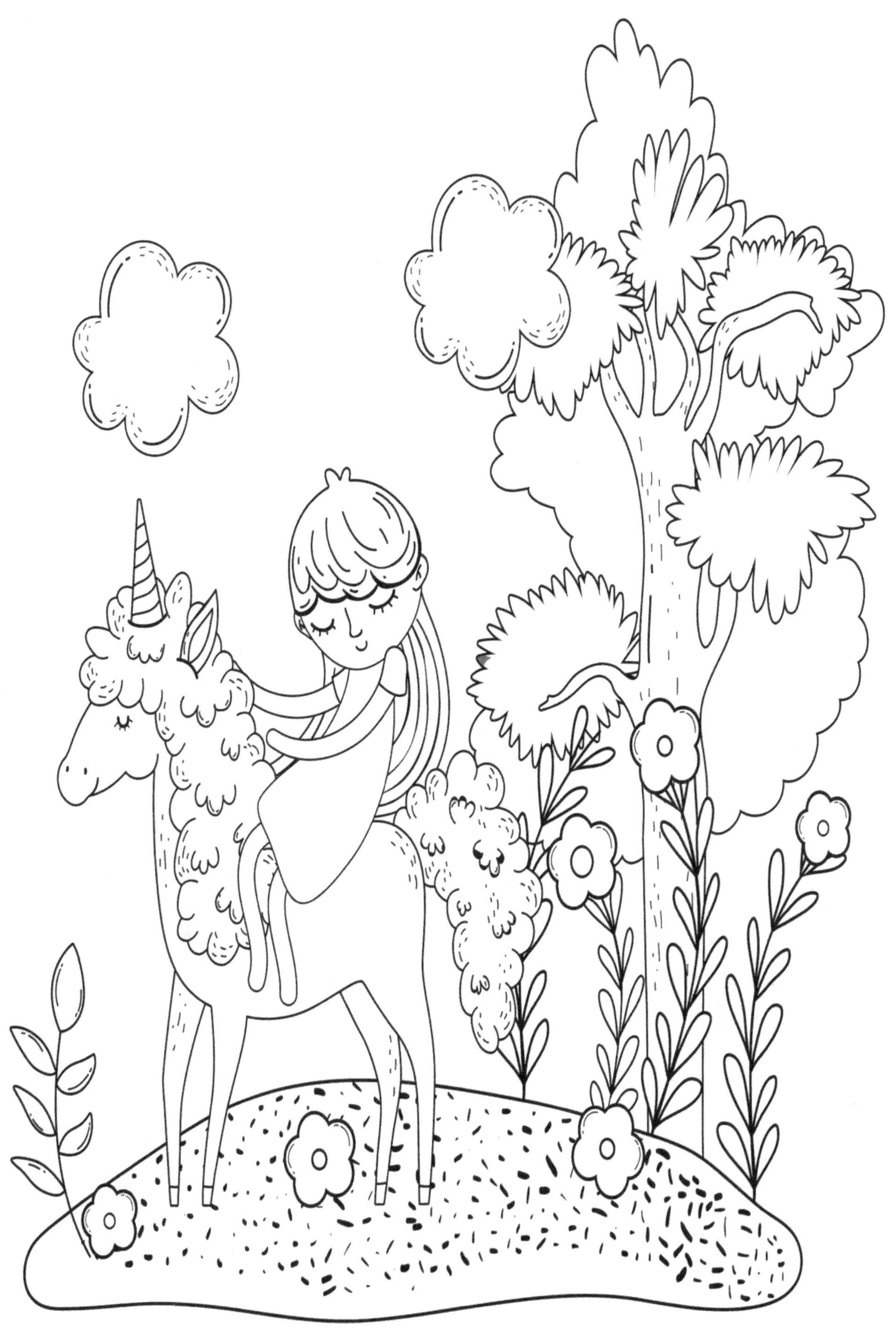

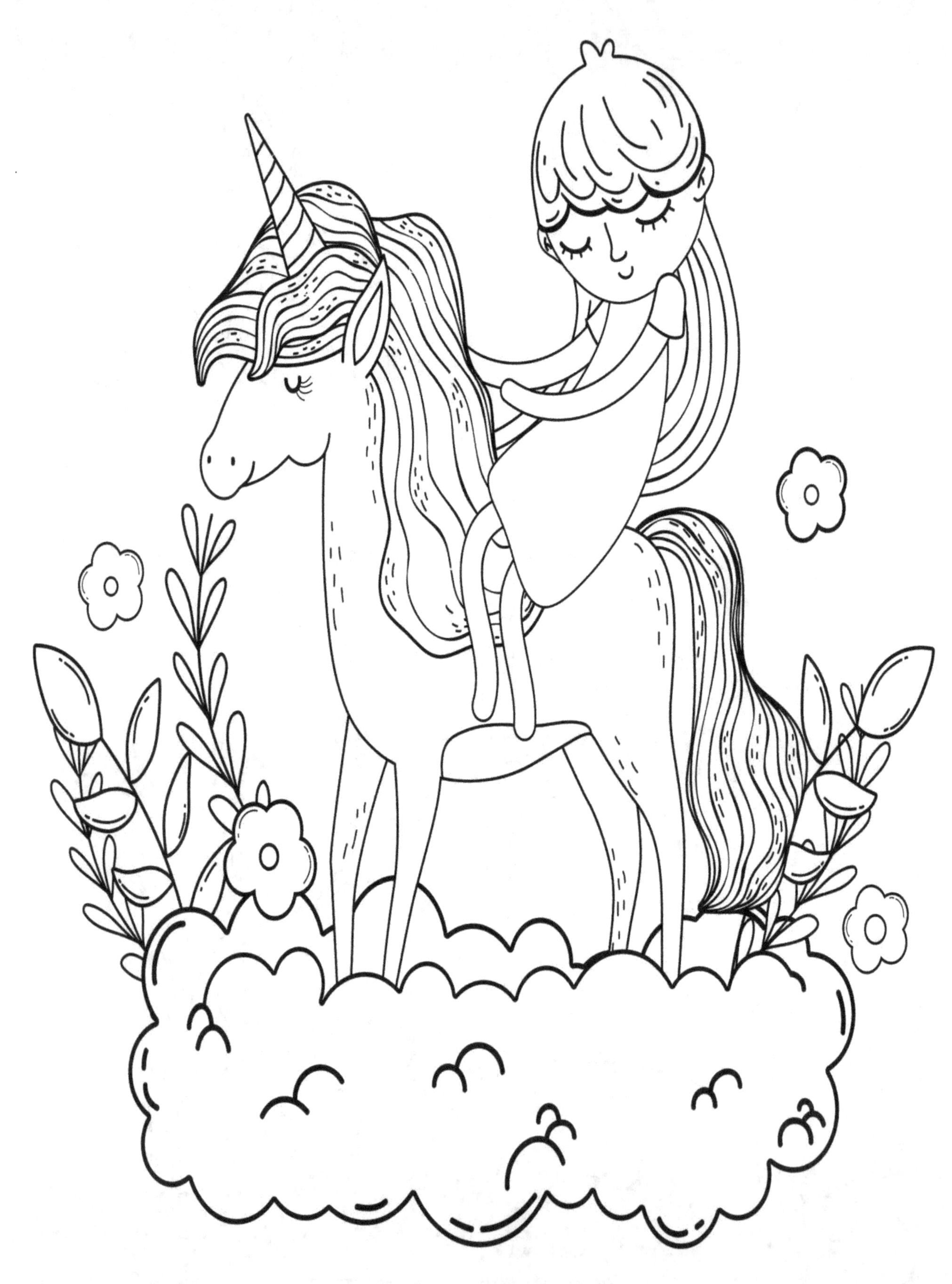

www.ingramcontent.com/pod-product-compliance
Lightning Source LLC
Chambersburg PA
CBHW080748120726
48001CB00009B/2707